Ghibliverse

Text and design © Carlton Books Ltd

First published in 2024 by Welbeck
An imprint of Headline Publishing Group Limited

Cataloguing in Publication Data is available from the British
Library

ISBN 978 1 80279 736 7

Printed and bound in China

Headline's policy is to use papers that are natural, renewable
and recyclable products and made from wood grown in well-
managed forests and other controlled sources. The logging
and manufacturing processes are expected to conform to the
environmental regulations of the country of origin.

Editor: Conor Kilgallon
Design: Russell Knowles
Picture Research: Julia Ruxton
Production: Arlene Alexander

HEADLINE PUBLISHING GROUP
A Hachette UK Company
Carmelite House
50 Victoria Embankment
London EC4Y 0DZ

www.headline.co.uk
www.hachette.co.uk

Ghibliverse

Studio Ghibli beyond the films

Books, music, manga and more:
a guide to a magical world

MICHAEL LEADER & JAKE CUNNINGHAM
Hosts of the GHIBLIOTHEQUE podcast

WELBECK

Contents

Introduction

Hello, and welcome to the Ghibliotheque. The podcast that leafs through the library of films of the world's greatest animation studio, Studio Ghibli...

That's how it all started for us, Michael and Jake, on the first episode of Ghibliotheque, back in July 2018.

Like an old married couple, we have our own special story of how the two of us got together. All those years ago, we were both working in the same office, and one day it came up in conversation that Jake, despite being a significant film fan, had never seen a single film by the legendary Japanese animation company Studio Ghibli. Not *Spirited Away*, not *My Neighbour Totoro*, not one from their peerless back catalogue of magical masterpieces.

Well, that just wouldn't do. Sitting across from him was Michael, an avowed Ghibli fanatic, and once he heard, his eyes lit up. He leaned forward and uttered the phrase that every twentysomething bloke wants to hear...

"Do you want to start a podcast?"

Cue the romcom montage. Hundreds of podcast episodes. Two pilgrimages to Japan. Road trips around the UK for dozens of film screenings, workshops and festivals. Interviews with animation legends, famous superfans and Ghibli veterans. And four books

Below: Posters for two of Ghibli's most well-known features *Spirited Away* (left) and *My Neighbour Totoro* (right).

covering Studio Ghibli, Japanese animation and Korean cinema.

All that leads to the book that you're holding in your hands right now, our fifth.

Hopefully the cover blurb has made this very clear, but just in case, let us spell it out: this is *not* a book about the films of Studio Ghibli. We already did that. It's called *Ghibliotheque – The Unofficial Guide to the Films of Studio Ghibli.* In that book, we dedicated a chapter to every one of the 20-plus feature films in the Ghibli library, following the story of the studio from 1984's *Nausicaä of the Valley of the Wind* (which was actually released before the founding of the studio, but was later folded into the catalogue) up to the present day, with Michael laying out the historical background behind the films and Jake offering up his considered analysis of the films themselves.

What attracted us to Studio Ghibli in the first place is not just that their films are of a uniquely high standard (although that certainly helps), it's that their work reveals to us the worlds and worldviews of the company's key creative talents, Hayao Miyazaki and Isao Takahata. However, as we've rewatched these films, spoken about them time and again, and shared them with audiences around the country, we have come to appreciate that, when it comes to Studio Ghibli, the

films contain multitudes, and their impact endures long after the credits roll.

By design and by admission from the filmmakers themselves, their work exists as part of a network of cultural connections that can lead you in all sorts of directions: deeper into animation, or somewhere else entirely – to the cinema, a bookshop, a concert hall, a theatre or a museum. The world of Studio Ghibli is a gateway to a whole universe of such experiences and epiphanies.

And so, in this book we're stepping out of the Ghibliotheque world and exploring *Ghibliverse: Studio Ghibli Beyond the Films.*

Whereas our previous books followed a linear, chronological itinerary, this excursion is expansive and sprawling, taking us away from cinema into various art forms and disciplines. Some of the chapters in this book are dedicated to aspects of the Ghibliverse which are as beloved and renowned as what you see on screen: the gorgeous, life-affirming soundtracks; the

Above: The two directors who shaped Ghibli, the late Isao Takahata (left) and Hayao Miyazaki (right).

Overleaf: *Totoro's* Mei and Satsuki skip with a blue Totoro creature in this piece of sculptural merchandise.

Above: Authors Michael (left) and Jake (right) introducing a screening of *Akira* at The Dukes Theatre in Lancaster.

Opposite: Ghibli films always feel perfectly assembled, and can even be enshrined in jigsaw puzzle form.

blockbusting stage productions; and the Ghibli Park and Ghibli Museum, two wholly unique endeavours that seek to recreate the magic of the films in the real world.

Other chapters journey to oft-unplumbed depths: surveying the "deep cuts" of the filmography, from shorts to music videos to documentaries; investigating the books written by and about Ghibli, as well as the authors whose work they've chosen to bring to the big screen; and tracing back the careers of both Miyazaki and Takahata to highlight some of the important works they made in the years before they set up their own studio, many of which still haven't been widely released – at least, not in our corner of the world. No matter how obscure or esoteric, it is all part of the Studio Ghibli story – and there are delights to be found.

We even answer the question that every self-respecting fan has asked themselves at least once: What does Totoro taste like?

Since starting this project in 2018, the films of Studio Ghibli have ventured into places unthinkable mere years before: onto the streaming services Netflix and HBO Max, and even to the top of the US box office charts, where Hayao Miyazaki's much-anticipated *The Boy and the Heron* found itself in 2023. After years of being a relatively niche concern, adored by English-speaking fans and switched-on families but still quite separate from the mainstream, they are now more available and accessible to curious audiences than ever before.

And what's exciting is that there is still so much more to explore, to learn and to enjoy.

Thank you for picking up this book. It has been a dream come true for us to delve so deeply into the ever-expanding universe of Studio Ghibli. We hope it serves as a star map to guide you on odysseys of your own.

Hello, and welcome to the Ghibliverse.

Michael and Jake

Somewhere between London, Sussex and Salford, with a new Hayao Miyazaki film playing in cinemas. December 2023

Before Ghibli

Did you think it all started with
Nausicaä of the Valley of the Wind?
Well, think again!

The Studio Ghibli story tells such a complete and compelling narrative that it's often easy to forget that both Hayao Miyazaki and Isao Takahata had already enjoyed long, eventful careers in the Japanese animation industry before the studio was founded. It's particularly easy to forget in the English-speaking world, where so much of their pre-Ghibli work still remains unreleased or overlooked. To many fans, Miyazaki and Takahata emerged fully formed with films such as *My Neighbour Totoro*, *Grave of the Fireflies* and *Spirited Away*, but there are many important works in the back catalogue: works that made their name, works that they personally held in great esteem, and works that bear the early glimmers of what would later be explored to great success in the Ghibli era.

The Little Norse Prince

Directed by: Isao Takahata
Length: 82 mins / Year: 1968

Studio Ghibli was formed in 1985, but the two directors who helped form the studio made their first film together almost 20 years previously.

Although it might not be perfect, *The Little Norse Prince* (also known as *The Great Adventure of Horus, Prince of the Sun*) marks the first feature film collaboration between Isao Takahata and Hayao Miyazaki, and for that reason alone it's deserving of a hallowed position in the halls of animation history. Having directed on the TV series *Wolf Boy Ken* (1963–65), Takahata had now graduated to the big screen, and looked to the past for his feature debut – as he would do for his final film *The Tale of the Princess Kaguya* (2013), which was an adaptation of the tenth-century folk tale *The Tale of the Bamboo Cutter*.

The Little Norse Prince began life as a myth, told by the indigenous Ainu community from Japan's Hokkaido region; it then became a puppet play called *The Sun Above Chikisani*, which was then adapted into the film. An episodic tale, the story follows a young boy on a quest to reforge an ancient sword. On the journey he encounters giant fish, scared villagers, terrifying wolves and ancient evils.

The younger Miyazaki had already formed a friendship with Takahata at a union committee meeting, and once production began, started sneaking drawings into his director's office – and soon found himself as a key animator, controlling entire scenes (learning on the job, Miyazaki says he "learned how to do that work during the process of making the film"). There are clear instances in the film where both filmmakers' skills and identities shine through. A splinter

being removed from a mythical monster links the natural and supernatural via grounded empathy – like the Stink Spirit in *Spirited Away* (2001) with its bicycle-shaped thorn in its side – and is emblematic of the studio's non-anthropocentric world view. A chorus celebrating a great harvest signals Takahata's lifelong fascination with and celebration of agriculture; and a gripping bout between Horus and a fish allows Miyazaki to give an early indication of his remarkable skills at staging action. But, due to soaring budgets and missed deadlines – something that would become a staple of Takahata's career – some of the most memorable scenes in the film are ones that are barely animated. Key moments, like a wolf attack and a rat infestation, are presented as simple slide shows, as time and money had finally run out to animate the set pieces. (However, in a strange way, the lack of violence does speak to the maker's moral pacifism.)

Muddled in its middle, as the character focus shifts and the propulsion behind Horus's various tasks starts to wane, *The Little Norse Prince* doesn't always make for satisfying viewing, but in moments it does sparkle with the nascent joys of its filmmaker's artistry. Ultimately, the film finally crawled to a release after almost three years of production, flopping at the box office but impacting animation forever.

Opposite: Sword play. Previously told with puppets, *The Little Norse Prince* is based on an ancient myth.

Yuki's Sun

Directed by: Hayao Miyazaki
Length: 5 mins / Year: 1972

Rarely considered as more than a footnote in Hayao Miyazaki's career, this curio enjoyed a brief surge in interest after the global streaming platform Mubi added it to their curated collection in late 2023.

In their editorial copy, Mubi billed *Yuki's Sun* as a "five-minute short" from Hayao Miyazaki, made 13 years before the founding of Studio Ghibli. Essentially a trailer-montage of evocative and dynamic scenes, this delightful and intriguing morsel was created as a pilot for a potential adaptation of the manga series by Tetsuya Chiba which, ultimately, went uncommissioned. For the diehards and the trivia obsessives, *Yuki's Sun* is also notable for being

Miyazaki's first work as a solo director, after previously sharing credit with Isao Takahata on a run of episodes on the 1971 *Lupin III* TV series. However, Miyazaki himself considers the later series *Future Boy Conan* (1978) as his true directorial debut.

Below: Fresh as a daisy. The pilot film *Yuki's Sun* marked Hayao Miyazaki's first solo credit as director.

YUKI'S SUN

Panda! Go Panda!

Directed by: Isao Takahata
Length: 33 mins / Year: 1972

Panda! Go Panda!: Rainy-Day Circus

Directed by: Isao Takahata
Length: 38 mins / Year: 1973

He's got a familiar smile, hasn't he, the panda in the image. An ear-to-ear, big, bright crescent moon of pearly whites – joyous, but ever so slightly unnerving as well.

It's Totoro's smile, the legendary grin that has charmed (and in some cases frightened) so many. Made famous by Miyazaki's *My Neighbour Totoro*, it was first brought to life under Isao Takahata's direction in 1972. It's a smile that belongs to Papa Panda, a panda who, along with his child Panny, has escaped from a zoo. The two stumble upon a house in the woods (all very Goldilocks) where they meet a young girl Mimiko, who's been left home alone, and who instantly forms an ersatz maternal bond with the pandas. Across two theatrically released brief adventures, the trio evade captors, get swirled into a drama at a dam, team up with a tiger and survive an apocalyptic flood, all in a combined total of 71 minutes!

There are a lot of recognizably Ghibli qualities in *Panda! Go Panda!* and its 1973 sequel *Panda! Go Panda!: Rainy-Day Circus*, ideas that are clearly percolating in these mid-length tales and which would be revisited once the studio was founded – and not just in works that came soon after (like *Totoro*) but decades after as well. From character designs to story elements

Right: Smile! The artwork for the 2022 American release of *Panda! Go Panda!* shows off Papa Panda's recognizable grin.

FROM ACADEMY-AWARD® NOMINATED DIRECTOR
ISAO TAKAHATA

PANDA! GO PANDA! © TMS

to train rides, these two works, although slight, show some deep-rooted artistic approaches that never leave Ghibli.

Even before Papa Panda arrives on screen, the opening titles of *Panda! Go Panda!* feel familiarly *Totoro*-esque: an orange background, layered with simplified rubbery characters and an undeniably catchy, peppy theme song. The following scenes – which feature fearless approaches to ghosts, some satisfying cleaning, a delectable meal and even the third-act drama of a lost child – balance domesticity with drama, giving the sense of a *Totoro* demo, albeit one where Totoro talks with a vaguely European accent and moves with the flexibility of a Hanna-Barbera cartoon.

Rainy-Day Circus is a grander story than the initial *Panda* tale, an action adventure built on spectacle and heart, in many ways a progenitor to that other child-friendly Miyazaki-directed favourite, *Ponyo*. In the first half of the film, an escaped tiger meets the panda family before being returned to its circus home,

and in the second a flood sweeps the landscape and threatens the local community. The circus is a joyously madcap location for Takahata's animators (who included *Whisper of the Heart* director Yoshifumi Kondō) to flex their skills, and to express the filmmaker's affinity with nature, both the tiger and its parent subverting expectations of fear. Later the flood sinks the characters into an ethereal, soothing tidal bath, reminiscent of the drowned world of *Ponyo* – with just the right amount of water for a train to glide across its shimmering surface, an image Ghibli would return to in *Spirited Away*.

Cartoonish and innocent, these two stories never attain the emotional heft of any Ghibli work, but as an exploration of creative genealogy they are both fascinating and very entertaining.

Above: Knock knock. *Panda! Go Panda!* opens a doorway for a fascinating peek at Takahata and Miyazaki's early work.
Opposite: Heidi, hi. Takahata's beloved *Girl of the Alps* series introduced viewers to a new style of animation.

Heidi, Girl of the Alps

Directed by: Isao Takahata
Episodes: 52 / Year: 1974

In our feature-obsessed, distribution-defined view of the careers of Isao Takahata and Hayao Miyazaki, it may seem that there was a fallow period following Takahata's troubled debut as director, *The Little Norse Prince* (1968).

As this chapter shows, he was far from idle, and in fact made some of his most impactful, influential and enduring works on television in the 1970s, years before the formation of Studio Ghibli.

Heidi, *Girl of the Alps* aired as part of the animation TV franchise *Calpis Comic Theater*, and was adapted from the beloved 1880 children's novel by Swiss author Johanna Spyri. It wasn't the first European work to be adapted – both Tove Jansson's *Moomin* series and Hans Christian Andersen's stories had been brought to the screen beforehand – but *Heidi* set a tone and style that would come to define the series as it blossomed into the long-running *World Masterpiece Theater*.

It was also the first to be made by Takahata, who by then had formed a tight creative bond with Hayao Miyazaki and Yōichi Kotabe, with himself as director,

Miyazaki leading on "scene composition" and layouts, and Kotabe serving as character designer and animation director. That bond had been formed on *The Little Norse Prince*, and continued once the trio left Toei Animation and embarked on other projects, including an ultimately unrealized adaptation of Astrid Lindgren's novel *Pippi Longstocking*, which informed the direction the team would take with both the *Panda! Go Panda!* shorts (1972–1973) and *Heidi*.

The opportunity to make Heidi came from the production company Zuiyo Eizo, and the creative team headed on a trip to Europe as part of Takahata's extensive field research. Alongside Spyri's story of a spirited young, orphaned girl and her idyllic adventures in the Alps with her grandfather, and her later struggles fitting into life in the big city, Takahata wanted to capture the culture, landscape and music of the setting, as well as offer a more naturalistic form of both storytelling and animation. "We were ambitious," Miyazaki later recalled. "We wanted to create a work for children that wasn't frivolous, and we wanted to break away from the compromised and slapdash television animation shows of that time."

Heidi was a hit, not just in Japan but abroad as well – but that success came with a cost. The team's exacting standards, coupled with the burden of producing 52 episodes a season, resulted in a hellish production schedule that required animators to pull all-nighters to satisfy the timeline: reportedly, later episodes had to be completed in less than two weeks each. "We stayed up all night for several nights in a row," Kotabe later recalled to Nintendo's Satoru Iwata. "I thought I might die. It was really awful." The mounting production costs saddled Zuiyo Eizo with insurmountable debt, which resulted in the company essentially dividing into two: Zuiyo Co. for the handling of *Heidi* and prior works, and the new studio Nippon Animation for the production of future series, including the next works by Takahata and Miyazaki.

In the documentary *The Kingdom of Dreams and Madness* (2013), Miyazaki singles out *Heidi* as Takahata's masterpiece, but he has always been clear-eyed about the dangerous and untenable production standards behind such a beloved work. That doublethink was reflected in the Ghibli Museum's 2005 exhibition about *Heidi*, which featured a huge diorama of an Alpine scene populated with clay

models and figurines, and a loving recreation of Heidi's grandfather's mountain hut, including the goat models that Miyazaki now keeps at his private studio and places out front for the amusement of local children.

The exhibition sought to showcase Takahata's research, Kotabe's character designs and art director Masahiro Ioka's breathtaking background artwork, all while exploring the herculean task of bringing this vision to television. "Takahata working on *Heidi* was the first to carry out such an exhaustive method of directing," Miyazaki notes, highlighting that his one-time mentor was able to succeed only because of the ambition and passion of the team, and that he fulfilled three conditions for undergoing such a punishing creative endeavour: "one is young, one is unknown, and one is poor".

Opposite: Swiss please. Heidi returns home for a special exhibition about the anime series in Zurich.

Above: A cabinet of Heidi merchandise on display at the *Heidi in Japan* exhibition in Zurich.

3000 Leagues in Search of Mother

Directed by: Isao Takahata
Episodes: 52 / Year: 1976

....

Having revolutionized the medium by offering a new form of television animation with *Heidi, Girl of the Alps*, the team were expected to perform the miracle all over again two years later.

Television animation is a punishing, insatiable industry, where success only encourages hunger for more content. Hayao Miyazaki remarked in 1987 that "television repeatedly demands the same thing. Its voraciousness makes everything banal". That's not to say that the follow-up series was any less successful, though – far from it. In Japan, it is held in high esteem, and it travelled far in foreign markets, especially in Southern Europe, South America and the Middle East. We're at a disadvantage in the English-speaking world, where the series variously titled *3000 Leagues in Search of Mother*, *From the Apennines to the Andes*, *The Heart* or, simply, *Marco* never caught on. Even

within this unsung period of Takahata and Miyazaki's careers, this is particularly unsung.

Whereas *Heidi* and the series that followed it, *Anne of Green Gables* (1979), were both adaptations of whole books, *3000 Leagues in Search of Mother* is much looser, expanding on a 10,000-word chapter of the 1886 novel *Cuore* (*Heart*) by Italian writer Edmondo De Amicis, a landmark piece of Italian children's literature. The series follows young Marco on a transatlantic journey from Italy to Argentina in search of his mother, who made the voyage years earlier to take up a job as a maid in a wealthy household. In adaptation, the story grew into a sociological epic that tackles themes of urban life, poverty and the plight of children. Reuniting Takahata with Kazuo Fukazawa, screenwriter for *The Little Norse Prince* (1968), this is a staggeringly ambitious work, complete with an expansive list of characters and communities that Marco meets over the course of his odyssey.

The lack of English-language distribution for *3000 Leagues in Search of Mother* has given us a skewed sense of where the series sits in Takahata's filmography. It's said that history is written by the victors, but in this case there's something different at play: history has been informed by those whose accounts have been translated into English. While it is another triumph for the

Opposite: As described in the chapter title of the original Italian story, Marco's journey takes him from the Apennines to the Andes.
Left: While journeying through Argentina, Marco meets the travelling puppeteer Peppino and his three daughters.

母をたずねて三千里

key team behind *Heidi*, this is also where the creative partnership began to fray. As with *Heidi*, the central creative team – Takahata and Miyazaki, now with art director Takamura Mukuo in tow – embarked on a research trip that informed Mukuo's rich background art, taking in the Mediterranean and, in particular, South America.

But once again, the production itself was a hard slog, and Kotabe recalls falling out with both Miyazaki and Takahata over certain sequences. Miyazaki, on the other hand, looks back on *3000 Leagues in Search of Mother* as something of a turning point for himself as a filmmaker. In a 1984 interview published in the collection *Starting Point: 1979–1996*, Miyazaki

describes the series as the epitome of Takahata's "everyday life animation – stories with realistic settings that place importance on everyday matters". While he clearly respects Takahata and his chosen direction, Miyazaki describes how their tastes "had diverged quite a bit", and within this style there were fewer opportunities for him to showcase his skills as a dynamic animator and layout artist. Ultimately, he realized he was more interested in stories rooted in fantasy and adventure than in real life. In his words, following *3000 Leagues in Search of Mother*, Miyazaki felt like he was "back to square one", and ready to embark on a new phase of his career, separate from his mentor.

Future Boy Conan

Directed by: Hayao Miyazaki
Episodes: 26 / Year: 1978

....

After decades of being unavailable (officially) in English-speaking territories, *Future Boy Conan* was released by the specialist distributors GKIDS and Anime Limited across 2021 and 2022, finally giving a landmark anime series its due prominence.

While not a huge success on its initial broadcast in 1978, Miyazaki's directorial debut has come to be seen as something of a Rosetta Stone for his whole career, described in a retrospective feature in *Animage* in 1990 as both a "culmination" of Miyazaki's prior work, and the "origin" of everything that is to come.

Miyazaki himself says that he took on the job of directing *Conan* reluctantly. Feeling disillusioned by Isao Takahata's move in the direction of grounded dramas, he wanted to work on something more action-packed, upbeat and fun after the serious themes of *3000 Leagues in Search of Mother* (1976). As he remarked in an interview in 1984, "I felt scared and troubled, but I didn't have any other option."

Japan's national broadcaster, NHK, had approached Nippon Animation, the company that produced *3000 Leagues in Search of Mother*, with the opportunity to create the network's first animated series, commissioning a 26-episode adaptation of writer Alexander Key's post-apocalyptic, young adult novel *The Incredible Tide*. By his own admission, Miyazaki disliked the book, specifically its blunt Cold War themes and what he perceived to be a bleak outlook for what he envisioned as an entertaining, hopeful series for children. And so, he used the original story as a "trigger" for the series. "I think of the project plan as simply being a vessel," he recalled in 1983. "Figuring out what to put into the vessel is part of my job."

In the process of adapting *The Incredible Tide*, Miyazaki retained not much beyond its post-apocalyptic setting, its core characters and civilizations. After that, he filled the vessel with ideas. The series follows Conan, a young boy and one of only two

remaining residents on Remnant Island, a small colony formed by survivors of a fleet of evacuating spacecraft that returned to earth after escaping a planet-devastating war. When a young girl, Lana, washes up on the beach, his isolated life changes forever, as he becomes acquainted with other human communities, including the verdant paradise of High Harbour and Industria, a dystopian society ruled by a power-hungry dictator.

While the series bears Miyazaki's authorial fingerprint, he wasn't entirely alone in creating the series. Miyazaki's former mentor Yasuo Ōtsuka was on board as animation director and character designer, and even Isao Takahata helped out with storyboards and episode direction on certain episodes. Dig into the credits and you'll find future Ghibli collaborators, such as key animator Yoshifumi Kondō, art director Nizō Yamamoto and colour designer Michiyo Yasuda, one of Miyazaki's most trusted colleagues. Dig even deeper and you'll find anime legends such as Madhouse co-founder Yoshiaki Kawajiri providing animation work and *Mobile Suit Gundam* creator Yoshiyuki Tomino contributing storyboards.

But there's a reason why this is seen as Miyazaki's first major statement. *Future Boy Conan* stands as the first expression of many of his pet themes: young characters acting in defiance of older generations, inheriting a blighted world where industry and nature are in constant battle, and striving for balance in their search for hope, all captured in an approach to animation

Opposite: *Future Boy Conan* pointed to a new creative direction for Hayao Miyazaki, before he ventured into feature filmmaking.

that is full of energy and zest for life, and crammed with spectacular sights both natural and man-made. Everything from *Nausicaä of the Valley of the Wind* (1984) to *Laputa: Castle in the Sky* (1986) to *Princess Mononoke* (1997) flows from here.

After working for years only in collaboration, Miyazaki had come into his own as a solo artist. Yasuo Ōtsuka, who had worked with Miyazaki for over 15 years, witnessed this change first-hand, describing it as like seeing a normal person turn into the Incredible Hulk. As quoted by Andrew Osmond and Jonathan Clements in their book-length appreciation of *Future Boy Conan*, published alongside the series' UK Blu-ray release, Ōtsuka remarked: "[Miyazaki had] accumulated tremendous experience. He combined great technique as an animator with an understanding of scenes and how characters should move. I was astonished. It was like working with a wizard of animation."

In 1983, Miyazaki himself recalled that in creating *Conan* he had experienced an epiphany of sorts, one

that helped distinguish his ideal approach to storytelling from Takahata's thoroughly researched, meticulous "everyday realism". Miyazaki wanted to entertain, enthrall and ultimately uplift audiences, transmitting his hopes for the future to the next generation. And rather than seeking to represent the real world in animation, he sought to use animation to create fictional worlds that have the integrity of something real. "Lies must be layered upon lies to create a thoroughly believable fake world," Miyazaki said. "And the people who live there should appear to think and act in a realistic way... The trick is turning the lies you create into a single coherent world."

While *Future Boy Conan* has been somewhat overlooked in the English-speaking world thanks to the quirks and frustrations of international distribution, its influence has been felt through multiple generations of filmmakers, both in animation and live action. Years before his success with the likes of *Memories of Murder* (2002), *The Host* (2006) and *Parasite* (2019), director

Bong Joon-ho used to binge the entire series of *Conan* while studying at the Korean Academy of Film Arts, later crediting it with teaching him "the concept of directing". More recently, in Masaaki Yuasa's anime series *Keep Your Hands Off Eizouken!* (2020), which revolves around a gang of girls who create their own amateur animation, the characters' greatest inspiration comes from thinly veiled recreations of clips from *Conan*.

Even within the dusty confines of the Ghibliotheque podcast, where we invite artists to share the impact of Miyazaki, Takahata and Studio Ghibli on their own creative lives, *Future Boy Conan* is sometimes elevated above the likes of *My Neighbour Totoro* and *Spirited Away*. *Steven Universe* creator Rebecca Sugar told us how they drew great inspiration from the series, studying the episodes to see how Miyazaki and his team achieved and sustained such a high level of quality in the demanding world of television animation. They also shared the series with the *Steven Universe* crew, and planted references throughout the show's run – most

overtly in the title of the episode "Future Boy Zoltron".

Then, Pixar director Enrico Casarosa revealed how he saw *Conan* at an impressionable age as a young boy growing up in Italy, and paid tribute to it in his feature film *Luca* (2021) by kitting out one of the characters in clothing similar to that worn by Conan. Less superficially, though, he used *Future Boy Conan* as a guide for his animation team, as an example of the kinetic energy that he wanted to bring to the characters in *Luca* – a quality he feels is specific to this era of Miyazaki's work. "There's a joy in the animation," he told us. "And a playfulness that I miss a little bit in the later work."

Opposite (above): Conan and Lana both have the adventurous spirit that reappears in future Miyazaki protagonists.

Above: Did you know Conan's outfit (left) inspired a similar look for part-human, part-sea monster Alberto in Pixar's *Luca*?

Anne of Green Gables

Directed by: Isao Takahata

Episodes: 50 / Year: 1979

The third series in Isao Takahata's trio of children's literature adaptations during the 1970s for World Masterpiece Theater (as the franchise was by that point officially called), *Anne of Green Gables* has the unfortunate distinction of being the one where the wheels fell off.

Adapted from Canadian author Lucy Maud Montgomery's 1908 novel about a young orphan who starts a new life among the remote, pastoral surroundings of Prince Edward Island, the series was beloved both in Japan and abroad, and is still highly regarded today, but it would be Takahata's last series under the *World Masterpiece Theater* banner and his final production for Nippon Animation.

The cracks had started to show during the making of *3000 Leagues in Search of Mother* (1976), but it's here that they fractured beyond repair. Animation director Yōichi Kotabe had departed, to be replaced by the rising young star Yoshifumi Kondō, but most notably,

Hayao Miyazaki, who had been Takahata's closest collaborator for a decade, left production after 15 episodes. Miyazaki had already made his directorial debut with the series *Future Boy Conan* (1978), so returning to Takahata's side as a layout artist may have seemed like a backwards move; and he'd be back in the director's chair soon enough with *Lupin III: The Castle of Cagliostro* (1979).

Opposite: The Japanese poster for the feature-length movie version of the first six episodes of the series.

Below: Takahata revisits Prince Edward Island, the inspiring setting of *Anne*, in the documentary series *Journey of the Heart*.

楽しもうと決心すれば、たいてい
いつでも楽しくできるものよ。

脚本・監督：高畑 勲

赤毛のアン
Anne of Green Gables
グリーンゲーブルズへの道

原作：ルーシー・モード・モンゴメリ

脚本：千葉茂樹／磯村愛子／神山征二郎　場面設定・画面構成：宮崎 駿
キャラクターデザイン・作画監督：近藤喜文　美術監督：井岡雅宏　音楽：三善 晃／毛利蔵人
声の出演：山田栄子／北原文枝／槐 柳二／羽佐間道夫
制作：日本アニメーション　提供：三鷹の森ジブリ美術館／スタジオジブリ／日本テレビ／ディズニー　特別協賛：日清製粉グループ
配給：三鷹の森ジブリ美術館

www.ghibli-museum.jp/anne/

清秀佳人

Anne of
Green Gables

"I love everyday life, and I think it's the most important thing... As long as you enjoy yourself, nature will bless you regardless of whether you are rich or poor. The sun shines and it rains. Flowers bloom and birds sing. It would be boring if you didn't enjoy those things in your life."

Future Boy Conan was at least partly to blame for *Anne*'s strained production. The series were running almost back to back, with *Conan* concluding in November 1978 and *Anne* premiering in January 1979. Much of Nippon Animation's crew was shared between those two series and another literary adaptation, *The Story of Perrine* (1978), creating a bottleneck that didn't allow a great deal of time to regroup and prepare ahead of *Anne*'s proposed year-long commission. Before long, there were insurmountable delays: episodes had to be dropped from the schedule, while others had to rely on flashbacks, limited animation and use of still frames in order to get over the line. The crew worked flat out, even through illness. Michiyo Sakurai, who replaced Miyazaki, recalls in the Blu-ray booklet for the series that she created her layouts while bedridden, and Yoshifumi Kondō reportedly refused to be signed off after contracting a life-threatening lung disease and continued to work right through his treatment.

It didn't help that Takahata's ambitious, perfectionist streak was in full effect. As with his previous adaptations, he embarked on an extensive research trip, this time with young Kondō accompanying him to Canada. However, more so than either of Takahata's previous series, *Anne of Green Gables* was envisioned as a remarkably faithful adaptation. Many of the episodes were named after chapters in the book, and Takahata pulled dialogue directly off the page. Kondō had proven himself as a master of exuberant, expressionistic character animation in *Future Boy*

Conan, but here he outdid himself with the quieter moments, finding a more realistic form of character acting, where emotions are expressed through subtle facial expressions and mannerisms – while his character designs, which transform through the years, ably capture the passage of time, as Anne grows from an unruly 11-year-old girl to a young woman on the cusp of adulthood. And throughout, the entire drama is expertly framed by the backgrounds of returning art director Masahiro Ioka, whose richly designed interior locations are as breathtaking as the sweeping landscapes.

Elements of *Anne of Green Gables* point to Takahata's later features – *Only Yesterday* (1991) in particular – and Takahata revisited the series with the release of a feature-length recut of the opening six episodes, distributed in cinemas and on home video under the Ghibli Museum Library label in 2010. It was for that release that Takahata reflected on *Anne* and his "everyday life animation" period, and perhaps summed up his worldview as a whole:

"I love everyday life, and I think it's the most important thing... As long as you enjoy yourself, nature will bless you regardless of whether you are rich or poor. The sun shines and it rains. Flowers bloom and birds sing. It would be boring if you didn't enjoy those things in your life."

Opposite: The character design of Anne was an important early credit for future Ghibli mainstay Yoshifumi Kondō.

Lupin III:
The Castle of Cagliostro

Directed by: Hayao Miyazaki
Length: 100 mins / Year: 1979

In our first book about Studio Ghibli, we toyed with the reductive notion of Hayao Miyazaki being Japan's answer to Steven Spielberg, but is there really much crossover between the two?

Porco Rosso (1992) is inflected with that rollicking *Indiana Jones* spirit, and Spielberg's *The Adventures of Tintin* (2011), hopping between set pieces, is similarly bursting with animation ingenuity, especially in a stand-out physics-defying motorcycle chase. Right from his first feature *Duel* (1971), for which the young Spielberg covered his hotel room with storyboards to plan that film's extended car chase narrative, it's been clear he knows how to bring cinema and vehicles together for maximum thrills. Much like Hayao Miyazaki. It's not always with airborne monsters or fantastical flying

machines that Miyazaki's pencil brings incredible momentum. In his own first feature *Lupin III: The Castle of Cagliostro* – a 1979 sequel to the film spin-off of an anime adaptation of a manga about a gentleman thief who gets embroiled in a counterfeit cash scheme – he takes the unassuming, classic, tiny Fiat 500 and turns

Opposite: Artwork for the 4K restoration of *Lupin III: The Castle of Cagliostro.* The gentleman thief continues to steal new hearts.

Below: Although action-packed, *Cagliostro* is full of moments to breathe – even if that breath is filled with cigarette smoke.

it into the vehicular epicentre for his action opener, with tyres clinging to cliff faces, bullets bouncing from bodywork and wads of wonga swirling across the screen. And, if you were to pick up certain home entertainment copies of Miyazaki's film, you'll find the film described on the cover as "one of the Greatest Adventure Movies of All Time", a quote attributed to... Steven Spielberg.

But, did he ever say that? Our research suggests not. Despite digging in every corner of the internet and scurrying through every interview we can, there doesn't seem to be any evidence of this trans-Pacific backslap, the only concrete link being in the Spielberg-produced *The Goonies* (1985), in which an arcade houses the Lupin-related game *Cliff Hangar* – featuring animation adapted from *Cagliostro*. That being said (or not, as the case may be), there is some truth to the quote. It may not be the "greatest" adventure film of all time, but Hayao Miyazaki's first outing as a feature director, hot off the success of *Future Boy Conan* (1978), did mark the arrival of one of the greatest adventure film*makers* of all time.

Within the boundaries of using pre-existing characters, Miyazaki remains original, using the cheeky, charming Lupin as an endlessly propulsive and malleable companion for audiences to experience his inventive, elastic animation. The plot sees the thief and his gang infiltrate the lavishly turreted gothic lair of an evil count-turned-counterfeiter, hoping to expose his scheme and return the castle to former glories. It's more cartoonish and morally simpler than any of the films that Miyazaki would make after, but is hugely fun, and is dotted with moments of breath and space – taking in the sight of clouds, or the taste of noodles – that would become staples of his work as a filmmaker.

Left: *Lupin III: The Castle of Cagliostro* is "one of the Greatest Adventure Movies of All Time". Says who?

Chie the Brat

Directed by: Isao Takahata
Length: 110 mins / Year: 1981

A stark and delightful departure from the stately, pastoral realism of Isao Takahata's adaptations of children's literature, *Chie the Brat* is a riotous comedy set on the hard streets of Osaka, following the life of an unruly young girl, Chie, and her do-nothing dad, Tetsu.

Adapted from the long-running "gag manga" by Etsumi Haruki, the film has a scrappy, cartoony style that befits the slapstick antics and outsize personalities at the heart of the story, but it has an underlying wisdom and wistful point of view on family life which points the way to Takahata's later manga adaptation, *My Neighbours the Yamadas* (1999) – a connection made all the more clear by both films using designs from Japanese *hanafuda* cards in their opening credit sequences. There's a link, too, with *Pom Poko* (1994), in an offbeat subplot that centres on the rivalries and bust-ups between neighbourhood cats, rendered as spoofs of yakuza and martial arts flicks, where it's claimed that a cat's prowess is linked to their testicles.

Chie the Brat was Takahata's first project to have no involvement from Takahata's one-time right-hand man, Hayao Miyazaki, but it is also something of a last hurrah for many of his long-standing collaborators who didn't make the jump to Studio Ghibli. Yasuo Ōtsuka and Yōichi Kotabe, who had both worked on Isao Takahata's previous feature, *The Little Norse Prince* (1968), served as character designers and animation directors, each focusing on and essentially assuming the roles of different characters: Kotabe as the young girl Chie and the alley cat Kotetsu, Ōtsuka as the layabout Tetsu.

It was Ōtsuka, in fact, who was reportedly approached by the producers first, with the request to lure Takahata into the director's chair following the conclusion of *Anne of Green Gables* (1979). Takahata agreed only after reading the manga for himself, but

once he committed to the project he was determined to do as much justice to scuzzy Osaka as he did to the picturesque settings of his previous projects. Painterly rooftop landscapes of Chie's neighbourhood were created by art director Nizō Yamamoto – who did follow Takahata to Ghibli, and worked on *Laputa: Castle in the Sky*, *Grave of the Fireflies*, *Only Yesterday* and *Princess Mononoke* – and Takahata took great pains to represent the idiosyncrasies of the Osaka dialect in the film, filling the cast with local comic actors.

In the promotional booklet for the release of *Chie the Brat*, Ōtsuka says the production was swimming against the current by focusing on everyday Japanese characters rather than superheroes, sci-fi adventures or fairy tales. They needn't have worried, though, as *Chie* was a success, and immediately inspired a series-length follow-up that aired on Japanese TV for 64 episodes. While at the time of writing the film unfortunately remains unreleased in the English-speaking world, that esteem back home endures to this day. If you happen upon an Osaka-themed capsule toy machine in Japan, you'll find inside tiny recreations of iconic regional tourist spots such as the Dōtonbori nightlife district, Osaka Castle and the tomb of Emperor Nintoku, right alongside a grinning figure of Chie.

Opposite: The Brat Pack. Chie and the Takemoto family provide the film with both hijinks and heart.

Gauche the Cellist

Directed by: Isao Takahata
Length: 63 mins / Year: 1982

As with all of Isao Takahata's projects from before his tenure with Studio Ghibli, *Gauche the Cellist* is a gem well worth discovering – if it ever receives official distribution in the English-speaking world, that is.

Adapted from a short story by writer Kenji Miyazawa (whose work also inspired Gensaburo Sugii's 1985 feature *Night on the Galactic Railroad*), the film follows a young musician as he struggles through rehearsals in advance of a concert. Over the course of four nights, he is visited by a series of animals, including a cat, a cuckoo, a tanuki and a pair of mice, and it is through his interactions and altercations with these creatures that Gauche develops a deeper sense of the connections between his life, his craft and the world around him.

While it was released after *Chie the Brat* (1981), this hour-long feature had been in production for five years – although, for once, that wasn't down to director Isao

Takahata's legendary love of working at a snail's pace. The film was made by Oh! Production, a small outfit founded by a team of veterans including Kōichi Murata and Kazuo Komatsubara, who were in-demand artisans in their own right, with credits between them on projects such as *Devilman* (1972), *Galaxy Express 999* (1978) and Takahata's projects throughout the 70s from *Panda! Go Panda!* (1972) to *Anne of Green Gables* (1979). With *Gauche the Cellist*, their ambition was to produce a piece of work of their own in the gaps between their team's commissioned work on other projects: a "long and thin" approach, as Murata himself put it.

In both Miyazawa's original story and Takahata's adaptation, *Gauche the Cellist* bridges the local and the global, the traditional and the modern, and the natural and the metaphysical. The struggling young cellist lives a simple life in a countryside mill house, where his daily practice routines are overseen by a portrait of Ludwig van Beethoven. He performs concert music with a local orchestra, but they're also employed at the regional cinema to accompany screenings of films (including send-ups of early animation). And yet it's through an awareness and communion with creatures great and small that Gauche finds his own talents and grows to understand the profound power of music. In an essay reprinted for the film's Japanese Blu-ray release, Takahata explains this criss-cross of themes and world views, encompassing music, nature and humanity, writing that "Kenji Miyazawa must have been envisioning a microcosm in which all the worlds were harmoniously integrated."

And so *Gauche the Cellist* plays out like a kind of children's fable. In the same essay, Takahata describes his intentions as follows: "Our hope is that children all over the country will watch this movie and experience the joy of music, while playing in the beautiful and fun world of fairy tales." Naturally, the success of such a thoughtful film rests on its execution, and versatile lead animator Shunji Saida excels at both specific details and delightfully expressionistic moments. He reportedly took cello lessons in order to get the on-screen representation of bowing and fingering the instrument just right, but there's also a wonderful looseness to some of the film's sequences, most playfully in Gauche's run-in with a local, tomato-stealing cat, who he riles and rattles with a spirited performance of the heavy, intense "Tiger Hunt in India", almost to psychedelic effect as the character design expands and warps under the effect of the music. This and other pieces in the film are original compositions by composer Michio Mamiya, who had worked with Takahata previously on *The Little Norse Prince* (1968), and who wrote the music for Gauche with his own uncle, a cello player, in mind. Notably, both Saida and Mamiya worked again with Takahata on his following feature, and his first for Ghibli, *Grave of the Fireflies* (1988).

Opposite: The Tanuki Sessions. If you thought Pom Poko was Takahata's first run-in with these furry creatures, think again...

Above: Tuning up. Over the course of these night-time visits from local wildlife, Gauche finds his muse.

Sherlock Hound

Directed by: Hayao Miyazaki (6 episodes)
Episodes: 26 / Year: 1984

....

The early 1980s were hard going for Hayao Miyazaki. Creatively, he had ended the 1970s on a high with both *Future Boy Conan* (1978) and *Lupin III: The Castle of Cagliostro* (1979), showing off his potential as a director, but as the new decade dawned, he found it impossible to get his own projects off the ground or over the line.

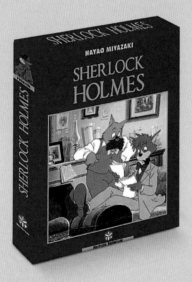

Instead, he made his final contribution to the *Lupin III* franchise by writing and directing two episodes of the TV series *Lupin the 3rd Part II*, both broadcast in 1980, and even found himself back at the key animator's desk for Osamu Dezaki's 1982 sci-fi *Space Adventure Cobra*.

Elsewhere, though, it was a struggle. For a brief time he was attached, along with Isao Takahata, to a long-gestating adaptation of Winsor McCay's comic strip *Little Nemo* (eventually released in 1989 as *Little Nemo: Adventures in Slumberland*). He found himself inspired by the fairy tale *Beauty and the Beast*, and produced image boards for a feature reworking of the tale, which were later published in book form as *Princess Mononoke: The First Story*. Another aborted project that drew from a similar wellspring of inspiration

was an adaptation of Richard Corben's underground comic *Rowlf* – a lurid fantasy starring a dog-turned-man-beast.

It's hard not to see some of these ideas reflected in the one project he did direct in this period, *Sherlock Hound*, a reimagining of Arthur Conan Doyle's master detective whose tales of deduction and derring-do take place in a turn-of-the-century Great Britain

Above: *The Adventures of Sherlock Hound.* A pair of DVD box sets from Pioneer's American release of the series.

Opposite: Miyazaki's take on Sherlock brought high-stakes adventure – and a canine makeover – to a familiar literary icon.

populated by anthropomorphic dogs and filled with steampunk-style flourishes that bear the influence of Jules Verne. Perfectly poised between *Future Boy Conan* and *Laputa: Castle in the Sky* (1986), *Sherlock Hound* finds Miyazaki in dynamic action-adventure mode, with richly drawn and vividly animated characters courtesy of designer and animation director Yoshifumi Kondô.

Miyazaki had big ideas for the series, including changing Sherlock's landlady, Mrs Hudson, into a younger woman with brains and an adventurous spirit of her own. He also wanted to reshape the way detective stories were brought to the screen, noting the following in a promotional pamphlet: "Even with Holmes, I didn't want him to be just a detective who takes credit for catching criminals... The most boring part of the story is probably finding the culprit of a crime that has already occurred." To that end, he brought on new writers who could bring fresh ideas of their own, including Sunao Katabuchi (*Princess Arete*, *In This Corner of the World*), who immersed himself in the whole Sherlock literary canon, including parodies and rip-offs, before giving the stories a unique spin: one full of kidnappings, pickpockets, flying machines and stolen submarines.

Of course, this being part of Miyazaki's cursed early 80s period, *Sherlock Hound* was beset with problems. Only six episodes had been finished before the Conan Doyle estate heard word and forced the production to cease. The issues were finally resolved, allowing the creation of a full 26-episode season, but by that point Miyazaki had moved on. A manga series he had created for *Animage* magazine had taken off, and he was in the process of developing it into a feature film: *Nausicaä of the Valley of the Wind*. Curiously, such was the delay that when *Nausicaä* premiered in March 1984, it shared screens with a package of two of Miyazaki's *Sherlock Hound* episodes as a taster before the show's broadcast in November later that year – providing something of a last hurrah for Miyazaki's TV-director phase, just as his feature career took flight.

Right: 221B Beagle Street. For all its animalistic embellishments, *Sherlock Hound* is still set in turn-of-the-century London – with some sci-fi flourishes.

2

Ghibli Deep Cuts

....

**Just how deep does the
rabbit hole go?**

Studio Ghibli may have an enviable canon of feature films, but these tell only part of the story. Dig further, and you'll find short films, TV series, video games, commercials, music videos and passion projects. They may be hard to track down, or even impossible to see without resorting to importing DVDs from Japan, but they play an undeniable role in the broader Ghibli narrative. This is where they let loose, let their hair down, and let younger or less experienced filmmakers take a turn in the director's chair. Together, they paint a picture of a studio that is rarely idle in between film productions, and which often uses these side projects as opportunities to experiment with new forms of animation and storytelling.

The Story of Yanagawa's Canals

Directed by: Isao Takahata
Length: 165 mins / Year: 1987

There comes a time in the life of every Studio Ghibli fan when they discover *The Story of Yanagawa's Canals*. Nearly three hours long, this is the infamous documentary about waterways which Isao Takahata made after producing *Nausicaä of the Valley of the Wind* (1984).

In fact, take Toshio Suzuki at his word, and the film plays an integral role in the Studio Ghibli story as a whole.

As reported by Yahoo! News back in 2014, Suzuki recounted that following the wildly successful release of *Nausicaä*, Hayao Miyazaki found himself flush with profits. However, he was burned out, and wasn't sure if he even wanted to direct another film – and he certainly wasn't interested in turning around a sequel. Instead, so the story goes, Suzuki suggested that Miyazaki use a portion of the profits to fund a project for Takahata to direct. And so, with the budget coming directly out of Miyazaki's own pocket (under his Nibariki production company), *The Story of Yanagawa's Canals* was born.

Miyazaki himself had visited Yanagawa – an area in Fukuoka Prefecture, on the southern Japanese island of Kyushu – and he recommended that Takahata visit the region to scout out locations for his own project. But Takahata never really did play by anyone else's rules. Instead, he was inspired by the city's historic network of canals, and the local community living beside them and fighting to preserve them. It turned out that he wasn't interested in making an animated film, after all; he wanted to make a documentary instead.

And what a documentary it is! There are short animated sequences peppered throughout, but don't expect high-flying adventure or dazzling moments of Ghibli magic. Animation is deployed only to illustrate the history and inner workings of the canals, such as an intricate sequence covering the waterway's network of dams, dykes and sluice gates that retain water while preventing flooding. For the most part, this is a slow, patient, observational film,

delivered at the relaxed pace of a gentle canal cruise, documenting the place, the people, and the tensions between tradition and modernity.

Takahata's films for Ghibli always contained elements that betrayed a documentarian's eye, be that the detours into safflower harvesting in *Only Yesterday* (1991) or the sequences in *Pom Poko* (1994) which use animation to explore how aggressive urbanization blights the landscape and destroys habitats, or even the obsessive detail in animating the simple act of slicing a watermelon in *The Tale of the Princess Kaguya* (2013). All of these tendencies are brought to the surface here. Thorough and exhaustive, this is hardly a breezy watch, but its themes are central to Takahata and Miyazaki's later film work, something best summed up by a motto that appears in the film: "Living with nature".

The Story of Yanagawa's Canals was also a typical Takahata production in that the director missed his deadlines and went way over budget, clearing out the coffers filled by *Nausicaä*. In a foreshadowing of their future partnership, Miyazaki had to shoulder that extra cost himself. To recoup the losses, Suzuki reportedly suggested that Miyazaki make another feature film, starting the ball rolling on the project that would become *Laputa: Castle in the Sky* (1986), the first film released by the newly named company, Studio Ghibli. "If Mr Takahata had made the movie within the time limit," Suzuki said, "*Laputa* would not have happened."

Opposite: Doc opera. Miyazaki suggested Takahata visit Yanagawa to scout out movie locations, but he made a documentary instead.

新文化映画

柳川堀割物語

やながわほりわりものがたり

宮崎　駿　製作
高畑　勲　監督作品

On Your Mark
(Ghibli Experimental Theater On Your Mark)

Directed by: Hayao Miyazaki
Length: 7 mins / Year: 1995

A rare short Hayao Miyazaki Ghibli film that was made available outside of the confines of the cinemas at the Ghibli Museum or Ghibli Park, On Your Mark (1995) is seven minutes of heaven.

Working within sci-fi, rather than his more familiar fantasy spaces (although this still very much has fantasy elements), the short follows two police officers as they try to free an angelic figure from a shackled, dystopian life. Set in a city built in an enormous underground silo, constructed due to a seemingly poisonous surface, On Your Mark sees Miyazaki collate imagery and ideas from his past, most notably Nausicaä of the Valley of the Wind (1984), and combine it with a new, futuristic setting. Equally intriguing is his experimentation with narrative structure, which results in perhaps his most illusive, yet still immensely satisfying, works of storytelling.

Made while Miyazaki was suffering from writer's block caused by Princess Mononoke (1997), On Your Mark was subsequently released in cinemas alongside Whisper of the Heart in 1995, its music provided by Chage and Aska, a pop rock duo who had appeared the year prior on the soundtrack to the Street Fighter film. The track itself is a shining artefact of its time, the wounded voices and towering guitars escalating to form a power ballad that would rival Bryan Adams' best, shaped with all the musical ambition and ear-catching hooks of Prince at his poppiest.

Beginning with our lead duo driving through reassuring green-grass and blue-sky backgrounds in a yellow Alfa Romeo (an image very similar to the opening of The Castle of Cagliostro, albeit with a slightly fancier Italian car), the film then descends into a dark, neon-trimmed city. It's thrilling to see Miyazaki briefly show his vision of a metropolitan dystopia, its endless glowing pillars of urban life, veins of Hot Wheels-like spiralling roads and eerie political signage recalling something as oppressive, cramped and cold as Terry Gilliam's Brazil (1985). In contrast to this fresh setting, the character designs show Miyazaki cribbing from his own worksheets, populating his city with people in ballooning radiation suits that look like Porco, cladding others in eye insignia common to the Nausicaä manga, and most obviously, the angel figure, who eventually climbs into the sky, spreading her white wings to appear just like Nausicaä and her flying machine, Mehve.

Fascinatingly, as the film reaches its seeming climax, a deadly fate befalls the protagonists. From here, events of the story are replayed but with a different outcome and no explanation given. A tunnel with a white light certainly suggests one answer, but Miyazaki suggests another, telling Animage magazine at the time, that the being could be seen as "hope". Perhaps this is how he arrived at the call to "live" against the odds in Princess Mononoke, and by creating a story that hinged on rewriting, he was able to get over his writer's block and write anew. Although producer Toshio Suzuki told anime scholar Helen McCarthy the studio didn't give the production "100 percent", it did allow them to experiment with using computers alongside hand-drawn animation, which would become part of Mononoke's production. And the thing is, when Ghibli isn't working at 100 per cent, they can still be better than most. Got a spare seven minutes? Get set, go.

Above: The two heroes of *On Your Mark* sat in front of their angelic companion. The stars of a short bearing Miyazaki trademarks and experimentation.

Above: Chage (left) and Aska (right), the duo whose music gives *On Your Mark* its foundational roaring ballad.

Commercial Break

Here's a tip. If you want to see Studio Ghibli at their most creative and stylistically diverse, import the *Ghibli ga Ippai SPECIAL: Short Short 1992–2016* Blu-ray collection. Not only does it include the *On Your Mark* music video in hi-def (plus several more videos for other acts), it collects Ghibli's commissioned work, including commercials for clients ranging from Nippon TV and Asahi Soft Drinks to the convenience store chain Lawson and the newspaper *Yomiuri Shimbun*. You might consider this "selling out", but it's how Ghibli kept the lights on between features, and the collection showcases the studio's ability to produce magical, evocative animation to order, even within mere seconds. These gigs also allowed their key talent to flex their muscles in ways they simply couldn't within a feature film framework. Pick it up to see bite-sized deep cuts directed by the likes of Hayao Miyazaki, Goro Miyazaki, Yoshifumi Kondō, Katsuya Kondō and, easily the most eclectic of the lot, Yoshiyuki Momose, who ably switches from Ghibli house-style to splashes of watercolour to experiments with computer graphics across his myriad projects.

Ghiblies / Ghiblies Episode 2

Directed by: Yoshiyuki Momose
Length: 12 mins (Ghiblies) & 25 mins (Ghiblies Episode 2) / Years: 2000 & 2002

....

How do you pronounce "Ghibli"? It's a question that has flummoxed fans the world over, and one of the many joys of the *Ghiblies* short films is that it's here where they inadvertently answer it.

Ghiblies Episode 2, which was released theatrically alongside *The Cat Returns* in 2002, opens with the iconic Studio Ghibli logo, only for the figure of Totoro to be replaced by the lowly office administrator Nonaka-kun, sitting at his desktop. He proceeds to tap backspace and promptly changes the Japanese text above the studio name from "Ghibli" (pronounced with a "j" sound) to "Gibli" (pronounced with a hard "g" sound).

Pronunciation aside, the meaning is clear: the Ghiblies of the title may be inspired by the staff at the real-life studio, but this is not quite the Studio Ghibli we know and love. Coming hot on the heels of *My Neighbours the Yamadas* (1999), the *Ghiblies* films play out as a series of fanciful sketches drawn from the mundanity of day-to-day business at the studio, like a comic strip come to life. The characters featured within are all loving caricatures of office staff, from the head of production, Oka-chan, who eats everything in sight, to the head of the publications department, the "hard-working career woman" Yukari-chan, whose untidy desk with enormous piles of paperwork is shown to resemble iconic mountain ranges from around the world.

Throughout, director Yoshiyuki Momose (a Ghibli veteran whose credits range from *Grave of the Fireflies* to *My Neighbours the Yamadas*) plays with the form, trying out different styles and even drawing back the curtain of animation production. The rough yet evocative character designs are based on doodles by the then president Toshio Suzuki – the exception being the character based on Suzuki himself, which was created by *Yamadas* author Hisaichi Ishii. In one brief interlude, we see how the animators behind *Ghiblies* tackled the problem of Oka-chan, whose entire face is obscured by a giant pig's nose. How is an ever-scoffing character supposed to eat with no visible mouth, anyway?

Elsewhere, there's a spirit of experimentation that makes it stand apart from almost everything else in the Ghibli canon. Some scenes are hand-drawn, others see characters drawn onto live-action footage, while others utilize Momose's experience as CG Director on *Princess Mononoke* (1997) to present rudimentary 3D computer graphics sequences, years before *Ronja, the Robber's Daughter* (2014) and *Earwig and the Witch* (2020).

The initial 12-minute short was broadcast on TV in 2000, and ends with a tease and a promise for the future: for all the high jinks, the real workers at Studio Ghibli are shown to be hard at work on their next feature film, due in 2001, which we now know as *Spirited Away*. *Ghiblies Episode 2* comes at a more substantial 25-minute length and is a much more assured, cohesive follow-up that works almost as a pilot for a Ghibli-themed workplace sitcom.

A delightful early sketch sees colleagues wrestling with the perennial question of where to get lunch, only to land on a local curry house with a diabolical gimmick: the spicier the curry, the cheaper the dish. Later, we see the workers close up shop for the night and head home, and follow Nonaka-kun as he travels on the train, only to miss his stop when a woman nods off on his shoulder and he becomes pinned to his seat. Nonaka is also the star of the film's standout sequence, an unexpectedly wise and heart-warming flashback to the character's first love. With its soft

ふと ふり返ると。

百瀬義行 監督作品

ギブリーズ

episode 2

西村雅彦・鈴木京香・古田新太/斉藤 暁・篠原ともえ・今田耕司/小林 薫

colours and nostalgic themes, this hidden gem in the Ghibli filmography pays loving tribute to Isao Takahata and his film *Only Yesterday* (1991), for which Momose contributed storyboards.

Far from throwaway, this deep cut deserves attention, and for all its gags and stylistic trickery, its intentions are disarmingly modest. Speaking of the *Ghiblies* project, Momose said: "The film we made isn't normal, and the characters aren't normal, but all we ever wanted to show was the normal everyday lives of characters who would be considered totally normal. My hope is that because of this film, people will take another look at their unchanging everyday lives, and

feel like they might be able to become the slightest bit more colourful."

And yet, this strange and small-scale curio has endured. Visit Japan, and you'll find *Ghiblies* merchandise sharing shelf space with characters from *Spirited Away*, *Howl's Moving Castle* and *My Neighbour Totoro*, from a cute little pin badge of Nonaka-kun to a soft plush doll of Toshi-san, the curry house chef, whose restaurant you can find recreated in the Children's Town area of Ghibli Park.

Above: School days. The most affecting moment of *Ghiblies Episode 2* is a tender flashback to Nonaka-kun's first love

Ghibli
Museum Shorts

Scarcity has always been central to the mystique and magic of Studio Ghibli.

For many years, the resistance against putting their films on digital and streaming platforms was believed to be a valiant defence against allowing their works to become seen as "content". Hayao Miyazaki himself has waged this battle for decades. He even grumbled when his films were first made available on home video in the 1990s, criticizing fans and families who obsessively rewatch his films. Instead, he recommended savouring the films with, at most, a single viewing per year.

All that has changed, of course, and yet, even now, when Studio Ghibli's films are widely available at a touch of a button, there is still a small corner of their filmography that remains elusive. They're not out of circulation, far from it, but in order to see them, you need luck on your side, and you have to put the work in.

The decision to screen original short films at the Ghibli Museum and Ghibli Park – and only there – is another act of defiance. A stand against a completist culture where checklists and bingeing are the norm. Not only do you have to travel to Tokyo or Nagoya, you have to give yourself over to the gods of scheduling, as only one of the ten films screens in each location at any

Opposite: The central entrance hall of the Ghibli Museum, with the Saturn Theater cinema in the background.

Below: Projector seat. One of the Ghibli Museum's exclusive shorts, as seen from the projection booth..

given time, and the listings are announced mere months in advance.

But what delights await you after that dice roll! Most notable among these exclusive films is the curious "mini-sequel" to *My Neighbour Totoro*, titled *Mei and the Baby Cat Bus* (2002), which follows the younger sister from the film on a short adventure with feline forms of transport small and large. Elsewhere, though, the exclusive shorts venture into new territory, with Miyazaki able to use the shorter runtime as an excuse to experiment between his feature projects, often testing out techniques that would later be seen on the big screen.

For example, the simple drawings and bright colours of picture-book adaptation *The Whale Hunt* (2001) and the colour pencil backgrounds of *Koro's Big Day Out* (2002) look ahead to the inviting stylization of *Ponyo* (2008), while the radical decision to use human voices to provide the sound effects in *Looking for a Home* (2006) would return in key scenes of *The Wind Rises* (2013). Not all of these shorts are looking ahead, though: *The Day I Bought a Star* (2006) revisits the visionary world of artist Naohisa Inoue (previously seen in *Whisper of the Heart* and *Iblard Jikan*), while *Treasure Hunting* (2011) is a second adaptation of the work of children's author Rieko Nakagawa and illustrator Yuriko Omura, after *The Whale Hunt*.

Like much of the Museum itself, the shorts are driven by Miyazaki's vision and imagination. Only one short, to date, has been directed by anyone else: the folk tale-inspired *A Sumo Wrestler's Tail* (2010), which was helmed by veteran Ghibli animator, character designer and animation director Akihiko Yamashita – although even that was based on a concept and screenplay from Miyazaki. Other shorts are pulled from aborted Miyazaki projects. The insect romance *Mon Mon the Water Spider* (2006) developed out of sketches for a film idea Miyazaki was toying with in the 1990s called *Boro the Caterpillar*, which itself was made into a short in 2018. The story behind that production, with Miyazaki coming out of retirement and wrestling with new CG (computer-generated) animation technology, was covered in depth in the documentary *Never-Ending Man: Hayao Miyazaki* (2016) – giving fans

Right: Keeping the mythological theme going, the screening room at Ghibli Park is called the Cinema Orion.

who aren't able to make the trip to Japan a glimpse at this exclusive work.

When addressing the Ghibli Museum staff at the tail end of 2005, Hayao Miyazaki explained his intention to recreate a "true film experience" with the Museum's shorts programme. "DVDs can be viewed over and over again," he remarked. "Watching films in this way makes it impossible to enjoy them the way they were meant to be enjoyed; it's a way to consume, or devour them... I think there's great meaning in creating an opportunity for us to experience seeing something just once."

There's great meaning, too, in creating an opportunity for us to experience *never seeing something*. At the time of writing, the Ghibliotheque team has visited the Ghibli Museum and Ghibli Park once apiece, across two trips to Japan in 2019 and 2023. Through a cruel twist of fate, the same film was playing both times: the delightfully barmy baking fantasy *Mr Dough and the Egg Princess* (2010). This glorious curio draws from Russian folklore in its depiction of the witch Baba Yaga, but immediately departs into its own eccentric and

extraordinary territory as she discovers a sentient egg-girl while cooking up a fried breakfast. The little egg is imprisoned, and is forced to tackle the witch's chores around the house until she pals up with a giant man made out of dough, who has been brought to life by magic. Together, they escape back to the egg kingdom and the girl is reunited with her royal parents – but not before Mr Dough is thrown into an oven, and emerges fully baked and full-bodied, offering up a Ghibli transformation like no other, and a short that simply must be seen to be believed.

Will we ever get to see the other shorts? Time will tell. Until then, we'll always have unfinished business with Studio Ghibli.

Below: Hayao Miyazaki in his 'atelier', a private building separate to his home and the Ghibli offices, where a lot of work gets done.
Opposite (left): Mei, Satsuki and the iconic Catbus, the Cheshire Cat feline public transport from *My Neighbour Totoro*.
Opposite (right): In a special short exclusive to the Ghibli Museum and Park, Mei meets a new friend, the Baby Cat Bus.

Hideaki Anno

Much was made of Hideaki Anno returning to the Ghibli fold to provide the voice of Jiro, the protagonist in *The Wind Rises* (2013). Perhaps the most successful of Hayao Miyazaki's protegés (more on that in Chapter 7: Next Ghibli), Anno had struck out on his own after working on *Nausicaä of the Valley of the Wind* (1984) and *Grave of the Fireflies* (1988). However, he did return to Ghibli for a trio of projects that are the deepest of deep cuts.

During a brief period when Ghibli had its own live-action subsidiary, Studio Kajino, it produced Anno's second non-animated feature, *Shiki-Jitsu* (2000), a challenging, self-reflexive arthouse film that starred real-life director Shunji Iwai (*Swallowtail Butterfly*, *All About Lily Chou-Chou*) as a disillusioned anime filmmaker returning to his hometown (Anno's own birthplace of Ube, Yamaguchi Prefecture) and meeting a strange young woman who seems disconnected from reality.

You'll likely never get to see Anno's second return to Ghibli, a short film titled *The Invention of Imaginary Machines of Destruction*, which worked as a companion piece to *Imaginary Flying Machines*, a Miyazaki-directed short that screened at the Ghibli Museum from 2002. Where Miyazaki's film presented an optimistic vision, Anno was tasked with the opposite: capturing scenes of destruction and devastation that played to the director's strengths.

Ten years later, Anno brought his career full circle, revisiting the fearsome God Warrior that he memorably animated in *Nausicaä of the Valley of the Wind* by writing and producing the short film *Giant God Warrior Appears in Tokyo*, a curious live-action "prequel" to Miyazaki's manga and feature film that depicted the events running up to the apocalypse. A co-production between Ghibli and Anno's own Studio Khara, the short premiered in cinemas in 2012, ahead of *Evangelion: 3.0 You Can (Not) Redo*, an entry in the big-screen *Rebuild of Evangelion* project.

The Night of Taneyamagahara

Directed by: Kazuo Oga
Length: 27 mins / Year: 2006

....

Studio Ghibli's home video distribution deal with Buena Vista Japan gave it a whole new channel for releasing smaller, niche projects.

One such release was the short film *The Night of Taneyamagahara*, released on DVD in 2006 and directed by Ghibli veteran and legendary art director and background painter Kazuo Oga, who contributed to films including *My Neighbour Totoro*, *Pom Poko* and *Princess Mononoke*. It was during the production of the latter film that Oga discovered the short story by Kenji Miyazawa (who also wrote *Gauche the Cellist* and *Night on the Galactic Railroad*), which tells a not too dissimilar story of the conflict between the human and natural worlds. A strange and at times confounding fable, *The Night of the Taneyamagahara* finds a man lost in dreaming and in nature, conversing with giant oak trees, small *kodama* creatures and the awe-inspiring god of thunder, and exploring a fundamental dilemma of human life: how to survive while achieving harmony with the environment. Like in *Princess Mononoke*, there are no easy answers, and a balance must be found between struggling to live and respecting the natural world. Essentially a picture book brought to life by narration and camera movements, the film highlights Oga's artwork and his skill at capturing rural life and the great outdoors: pools of light and colour around a campfire at night, morning haze and mist over the mountains, skies filled with countless stars. All spaces where the human and the divine can co-exist.

Iblard Jikan

Directed by: Naohisa Inoue
Length: 30 mins / Year: 2007

Released by Ghibli as part of their *Ghibli ga Ippai* collection, Iblard Jikan is another short film that salutes a gifted artist and their distinctive work.

Naohisa Inoue provided the extraordinary background artwork for the imaginary world dreamed up by Shizuku in *Whisper of the Heart* (1995) – the landscapes that her character and the dashing Baron traverse in the film's fantasy sequences. The artist also lent his voice to one of the charming old blokes who accompany Shizuku and Seiji in their impromptu rendition of 'Take Me Home, Country Roads', but here, Inoue serves as director, bringing to screen the rich creative world that he had been exploring and mapping out since the early 1980s in picture books, comics and paintings.

More of a gallery piece than a narrative short film, *Iblard Jikan* progresses as a series of dialogue-free vignettes as the camera passes over Inoue's evocative painted landscapes. It's an exercise in world-building, and what a world it is. Like the prog rock album covers of Roger Dean, these images present intriguing, inviting worlds that excite the imagination. Humble, pastoral scenes mingle with sci-fi flourishes: cosy settings of cottages alongside streams are revealed to be framed by otherworldly colours and structures, or overshadowed by giant planetary bodies looming over the horizon. Inoue's idiosyncratic vision is at times verdant, vivid and unreal, imagining a sort of impressionistic retrofuturism, with French market towns overseen by outlandish zeppelins. It's a world, and a way of seeing, in which you could easily – and happily – lose yourself.

Opposite: Tree of Life. The DVD cover of *Night of Taneyamagahara* foregrounds the connection between humanity and nature.

Above: Art Movie. *Iblard Jikan* is a dazzling montage of breathtaking vistas and vignettes by Naohisa Inoue.

NiNoKuni

Directed by: Yoshiyuki Momose
Length: 106 mins / Year: 2019

....

There is magic in *NiNoKuni* (2019), the kind with sorcerers, flying beasts and portals, but that ineffable, pervading Ghibli magic, the kind that seems to envelop a film's entire world, dousing its details in transformative, tangible fantasy and simplicity – it doesn't quite have that.

Adapted from a video game franchise that began with 2010's *Ni no Kuni: Dominion of the Dark Djinn*, the film is a curio of Ghibli connection, both unrelated to the studio and completely bound to it. Although Hayao Miyazaki is reportedly not a fan of video games, Ghibli producer Toshio Suzuki, like most producers, is a fan of getting his company work. So once production was wrapped on 2008's *Ponyo* and his animators were sitting around twiddling their thumbs, he got them working on the first *Ni no Kuni* game, which was being made by game developer Level-5 for the Nintendo DS (though there have since been reversions for alternate consoles and world-expanding mobile games). It's a role-playing game set between our world and a fantasy domain, and Ghibli supplied animation directed by Yoshiyuki Momose, who had been at the company since *Grave of the Fireflies* (1988) and was a key animator on *Spirited Away* (2001). The Ghibli connection to the game doesn't stop there; composer Joe Hisaishi, similarly fresh from *Ponyo*, joined the production too, perhaps making the project the closest audiences could get to a Ghibli video game. It was a critical and commercial success, and a direct sequel *Ni no Kuni II: Revenant Kingdom* was released in 2018, and in 2019 a film was announced. In the director's chair: Momose.

As well as working on the *Ni no Kuni* games, Momose had worked in the interim on Ghibli's *The Tale of the Princess Kaguya* (2013) and had directed a segment of Studio Ponoc's 2018 anthology film *Modest Heroes*. His section, the awkwardly titled "Life Ain't Gonna Lose", about a young boy with a severe egg

allergy, signalled an empathetic, expressive filmmaker ready to splash around with colours and screen space with emotional abandon. Unfortunately, despite his longstanding connection with the Ni No Kuni source material, and indications of experimental ambition, Momose's feature isn't the heartfelt, fresh adaptation one might hope for.

Following two boys who hold up two sides of a teenage love triangle, it begins as a modern YA melodrama, but after a car crash ports its leads into the mysterious kingdom of Evermore, it adds a medieval twist to the battles of adolescent romance. Dog-faced drunkards, green-skinned baddies and walking, talking plush dolls fill this other world, one that is being torn apart by war. While the character design is creative, and the imaginative, detailed and sun-drenched backgrounds are impressive, NiNoKuni never becomes truly transportive. Its relentless plot, crammed with world-switching, curses, reveals, several instances of deus ex machina and endless exposition leaves little

time to get comfortable. Hisaishi's score trots along with a sense of curiosity and wonder, but the project ultimately results in a restless film, overburdened with trying to reroute the exploratory, expansive feeling of a video game onto rails of linearity and getting lost along the way.

Opposite: Japanese poster for NiNoKuni showing its three lead characters and the otherworldly setting of Evermore.

Above: Although its story isn't the most beautifully executed, NiNoKuni's fantasy setting is an undeniably striking place.

Ronja,
The Robber's Daughter

Directed by: Gorō Miyazaki
Episodes: 26 / Year: 2014

Here at Ghibliotheque, we're fully paid-up Gorō Miyazaki apologists. Between his work designing and overseeing the Ghibli Museum and Ghibli Park, and his three feature films as director, he has played a significant and often undervalued role in the recent history of the studio.

Many of these projects were started under the urging of Toshio Suzuki, the producer that Gorō Miyazaki once described on our podcast as "a dark wizard" who is "very good at making people do what he wants them to do" – and that's still the case with *Ronja, the Robber's Daughter*, a corner of the Ghibli filmography that is a fascinating mix of the new and the familiar.

It was Miyazaki who had happened upon the source novel, written by *Pippi Longstocking* author Astrid Lindgren, when he was looking for potential projects to adapt. He was reportedly inspired, as a new dad, by the book's depiction of a relationship between a young girl and her bandit chief father, as she gains independence and goes on her own adventures in the verdant forests of medieval Scandinavia, observing the changing of the seasons and encountering the magical and mysterious creatures that call the woodlands home.

By approaching Lindgren's work, the younger Miyazaki found himself stepping on his father's

Opposite: Director Gorō Miyazaki was drawn to the depiction of a father-daughter relationship in Astrid Lindgren's source novel.

Below: Sticking together. On her adventures, Ronja meets new acquaintances and accomplices, such as her best friend, Birk.

toes. As was the case with Ursula Le Guin and her Earthsea stories, Hayao Miyazaki had been refused permission when he and Isao Takahata had attempted to adapt *Pippi Longstocking* into an animated series in the 1970s. Would Gorō once again be working in Hayao's shadow?

Toshio Suzuki, as always, had a plan. As related by Gorō Miyazaki at a press conference for the *Ronja* series, Suzuki's diabolical scheme was to try something that his old colleague would never dream of doing: using CG animation. Not only would this be Ghibli's first production in this style, it would also be their first television series: a format that the studio's founders had once excelled at, but consciously left behind for good.

And so, with a few key Ghibli regulars in tow, including character designer Katsuya Kondō, composer Satoshi Takebe and background artists Yoshikazu Fukutome and Sadaaki Honma, Miyazaki collaborated with CG animation company Polygon Pictures, an outfit that had already made a mark on productions across film, television and video games, ranging from *Ghost in the Shell 2: Innocence* (2004) to *Star Wars: The Clone Wars* (2011–2013).

Rather than a fully CG aesthetic (as seen in Miyazaki's subsequent feature, *Earwig and the Witch*), *Ronja* was produced in a hybrid style, with cel-shaded computer-animated characters set in front of hand-painted backdrops. As with *Earwig*, it's at times disconcerting to see Kondō's distinctive character designs applied to 3D figures, but *Ronja*'s lush natural landscapes give the series the edge over the later feature. In a hat tip to Takahata and Miyazaki's television work in the 1970s, priority was given to research into the history and environment of Scandinavia, while the unhurried storytelling also harks back to the likes of *Heidi, Girl of the Alps* (1974) and *Anne of Green Gables* (1979). However, despite landing distribution deals with broadcasters around the world – even, notably, a version translated into Scottish Gaelic for BBC Alba – and receiving a fair amount of acclaim from critics and the industry, including winning an International Emmy for Kids Animation, *Ronja* never quite scaled the heights of its forebears.

Overleaf: Hybrid Theory. On *Ronja*, Gorō Miyazaki used a mix of 3D characters and gorgeous painted backgrounds.

Zen – Grogu and Dust Bunnies

Directed by: Katsuya Kondō
Length: 3 mins / Year: 2022

The short-lived Studio Ghibli official Twitter account didn't have to work hard to get engagement. Social media had given Ghibli lovers worldwide a direct line to their beloved animators.

Whether it was a cryptic detail about an upcoming release, a schematic for a Ghibli Park attraction, or sometimes just a still from a film we've all seen thousands of times, every Ghibli tweet got fans talking. However, few Ghibli tweets caused such wild speculation as when they shared the logo of another film studio, a galactically popular one: Lucasfilm.

Why would they tweet it? Was Porco Rosso about to join the Rogue Squadron? Was another lucrative streaming deal about to be announced? Like Studio Trigger (*Promare*) or Ireland's Cartoon Saloon (*Song of the Sea, Wolfwalkers*), was Ghibli going to be producing a chapter of Lucasfilm's animated *Star Wars* anthology show *Visions* (2021–)?

No, it was something totally out of the purple-blue skies of Tatooine: a three-minute film about the industrial level meme-making *Mandalorian* star Baby Yoda (officially named Grogu, if you're insisting), just kind of, sitting around, playing with Ghibli's Soot Sprites, the silent and spherical, house-haunting, bath-house dwelling creatures who appear in both *My Neighbour Totoro* (1988) and *Spirited Away* (2001).

At its simplest, *Grogu and Dust Bunnies* is a short, sweet animation that takes the cute, wide-eyed mascot of one studio and throws it into a hand-drawn playground from another. A tan, papyrus-like background gives the short a sepia sense of history, as if we've unrolled a scroll from a long, lost crossover episode. Directed by Ghibli key animation stalwart Katsuya Kondō, 2D Grogu is rendered softly and simply, the animator's observant lines finding the slow stretches and quick bounces of trepidation and excitement as acrobatic Dust Bunnies discover and dance around their new extraterrestrial friend. They also hand a plant to Grogu, recalling a similar gesture of companionship from Ghibli's 1986 film *Laputa: Castle in the Sky* (which Kondō worked on), and, true to Ghibli form, underlines the connective power of nature.

Accompanying the playful characters comes a score from blockbuster maestro of the moment Ludwig Göransson. Leaving pulsating bombast to his scores for *The Mandalorian* (2019–), *Black Panther* (2018) and *Tenet* (2020), his music here is gentle and warming, finding the cosmic in a mix of ambience and sparkling synths like those of pioneering Japanese electronic composer Isao Tomita.

So, despite only being three short minutes long, there is more to *Zen – Grogu and Dust Bunnies* than just a brand collaboration. The fact that Lucasfilm unravelled any narrative binds to the *Star Wars* canon, to allow this free-wheeling, expressive burst of creativity to exist, shows the powerful prospect that a Ghibli partnership can have – although who knows, maybe this means that one day *Totoro* and *Spirited Away* will get retconned to exist in a galaxy far, far away.

Opposite: The force (of a humongous film studio collaboration) is strong with this one. *Zen* brought Ghibli into *Star Wars* and on to streamer Disney+.

Ghibli Music

Of all the many magical
qualities of Studio Ghibli's films,
its music has a special hold on
fans the world over.

At the heart of it all is composer Joe Hisaishi's decades-spanning work with Hayao Miyazaki, a partnership that rivals the great collaborations of film history. If Miyazaki is Japan's answer to Steven Spielberg, Joe is his John Williams – a genius in his own right, who reaches a whole new level when paired with Miyazaki. Joe's sweeping scores capture the heart, while his pristine, catchy melodies stick in the head for days on end. Miyazaki may be a wizard on the animation front, but Joe is his match when it comes to music. These soundtracks play an integral role in how the films of Studio Ghibli worm their way into our lives, and they're essential to the sense that the Studio's films are something unique, but universal; idiosyncratic, yet inspired; virtuosic and virtually impossible to imitate.

The Maestro of Studio Ghibli

The audio identity of the studio can be found in composer Joe Hisaishi's scores

···

When Netflix bought the rights to Ghibli's films, it made the films more accessible than ever. New audiences could discover them, old fans had another way of re-watching them.

They had gone from exclusivity to inclusivity – if you can afford an ever-increasing subscription cost of course. Making the step into streaming changed people's relationships to Ghibli. With a few clicks, and without even leaving the sofa, a library of films was available. It was a banner day, but there's another streaming deal that got Ghibli fans very excited, the one for Joe Hisaishi's scores. Having been released on vinyl, cassette and CD, the music by the man who for many has defined the sound of Studio Ghibli, was now just a click away too.

For some writers, who might struggle to type to the sound of lyrics, film soundtracks are an essential tool for getting words on the page. Right now, these words

are appearing on this page thanks to the score to *Porco Rosso* (1992) playing via Spotify, which (along with the vast majority of the studio's scores) appeared on the service in February 2020. Since then, Ghibli's music, and especially the work of Joe Hisaishi, has been a constant in our listening lives, to the point that in terms of time, we have committed considerably more to Joe's music than watching the films. These scores make writing a pleasure and are a pleasure to write

Opposite: While Hayao Miyazaki is Ghibli's foremost genius, Hisaishi's scores have made him a beloved musical icon.

Below: *Porco Rosso* gets a big thumbs up from fans for its action and adventure thrills, but its score is equally worthy of praise.

about. They glide from wobbling neon synths, to chest-pumping orchestral bombast, to delicate and almost privately intimate piano melodies. If the filmmakers build the planes, Joe adds the fuel, and together they take flight.

Hisaishi's collaboration with Hayao Miyazaki began with *Nausicaä of the Valley of the Wind* (1984) and continued across four decades, all the way up to 2023's *The Boy and the Heron* – and, hopefully, beyond. In that time he has created some of the finest film music ever made. Hisaishi has a remarkable gift for scale and melody – rivalled only by that other titan of the film score, John Williams – plundering his orchestra for sweeping sounds that fill establishing shots with the awe and wonder of discovering a new world, and in the process creating an earworm that will not dislodge for months (listen to *Princess Mononoke* from 1997 to hear Joe at his most epic and most hummable). That first score, for *Nausicaä*, is a lovely fusion of the electronic style of Hisaishi's youth, fused with the soaring orchestration he'd go on to be more known for. The synth lines and crunchy, high-tempo drumbeats might seem anachronistic, but in Nausicaä's dystopian world – one where technological evolution forced a future world to crumble into a more archaic setting – they seem to fit, the score's melancholy pop quality contrasting the hero's optimism with her poisoned surroundings.

Laputa: Castle in the Sky (1986) brings more pomp, an early, earnest trumpet solo proclaiming the film's honest valour, while later soft woodwind lines reveal an older sibling to the melodies that would define *My Neighbour Totoro* two years later. Dialled towards a younger crowd, the music of *Totoro* is full of vibrant, lilting moments and playful instrumental surprises, with orchestration, synths, samples and vocals dancing though singalong simplicity, otherworldly eeriness, hankie-grabbing delicacy and big band joy (which the *Totoro* stage show wonderfully showcased, see page 110). Films full of exploration (both in the air, and in the self), *Kiki's Delivery Service* (1989) and *Porco Rosso* feature scores that are full of adventure and pathos: flutes ripple with excitement alongside introspectively tinkling light keys, the surprising, waltzing instrumentation making for transportive, suitably European, listening. Miyazaki's work in the late '90s and early 2000s, from

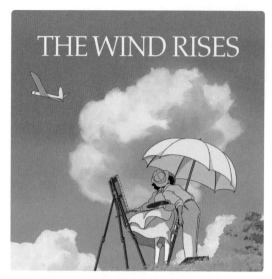

Princess Mononoke to *Spirited Away* (2001) to *Howl's Moving Castle* (2004), leads to the most recognizably "blockbuster" sound for Hisaishi. Drums thump deeper and strings swell sweeter. The three films, with their elusive morality and dreamy settings, are pushed into more ethereal territory, with large vocal groups deployed to underline both the spiritual and barbaric – angelic choirs and violent, battling clans. Hisaishi then returns to that bouncing, yet complex, innocent dynamism of *Totoro* with *Ponyo* (2008), a film built around a character intended to compete with Totoro on the cuteness scale. Diving from a squeaky clean pop theme through Wagnerian enormity and into rosily romantic opera, it's perhaps Hisaishi's most joyous score.

Despite this huge output of remarkable works, Hisaishi's finest year wouldn't arrive until 2013, when he scored his tenth film for Hayao Miyazaki and his first (and sadly only) for Isao Takahata. Intended to be released together, *The Wind Rises* and *The Tale of the Princess Kaguya* see three artists working at the top of their game, and the two resulting scores are constantly battling for top position on our Hisaishi ranking. *The Wind Rises*, which opens with a delightfully wistful mandolin, eases into melancholy and nostalgia via thoughtful plucked strings, before elegantly navigating war and romance with passion and tragedy, never explosives. It's gentle, rousing, spine-tingling and heartbreaking, ideally suited to the film's multifaceted protagonist Jiro. With *The Tale of the Princess Kaguya*,

Hisaishi was starting fresh with his director. The result, perhaps unsurprisingly, is something entirely different to anything he'd done before. Sparse, modern and deeply moving, echoing the director's approach of putting only the essential on screen, the score is spacious but hugely impactful. It builds from light piano rolls and intermittent chimes, to joyous, lush string suites pinched with sadness, to the off-kilter percussive jangles and hollers of a parade. It's unlike any of his previous work, and its influence can be heard ten years later, in *The Boy and the Heron*. Starker than any of his other Miyazaki scores, the piano-led work is, like protagonist Mahito, searching and sad; the standout track 'Ask Me Why' grounds lofty animation in lonely repetition, gradually shifting hopewards. It's a stripped-back piece that perhaps shows what makes Hisaishi so skilled in the first place. He can work with electronics or an orchestra, but whether he's solo or accompanied, he unlocks the magic of Ghibli like nobody else.

Above (left): Chart Topper. Joe Hisaishi's *Symphonic Celebration* album was a runaway smash hit on its release in 2023.

Above (right): *The Wind Rises* was Joe Hisaishi and Hayao Miyazaki's tenth feature collaboration in a row.

Opposite (above): To hear Joe's genius in full effect, listen to his scores for *The Wind Rises* and *Princess Kaguya*, recorded in the same year.

Opposite (below): The Waterwheel Turns. After almost 30 years of scoring Miyazaki's films, Hisaishi finally worked with Isao Takahata on *Princess Kaguya*.

Joe Hisaishi: Live!

Joe Hisaishi Symphonic Concert: Music from the Studio Ghibli Films of Hayao Miyazaki.

....

In the time between Joe Hisaishi announcing the London dates of his "symphonic concerts" to actually performing them, Studio Ghibli went from secretive tinkerers to having two new recent releases under their belt (2020's *Earwig and the Witch* and 2023's *The Boy and the Heron*).

Having rightfully delayed and delayed due to the COVID-19 pandemic, Joe was struck down by the virus just before his scheduled performances in 2022. So, having traversed the globe, he finally took to the stage of Wembley Arena a year later, in September 2023 – to be met by 25,000 elated Ghibli fans.

David Bowie, Whitney Houston, the Rolling Stones. All had played here, and with this performance (both on the keys or conducting the BBC Concert Orchestra and Crouch End Festival Chorus) Joe Hisaishi demonstrated that his heart-swelling, electrifying work is in tune with the musical royalty who had stepped on stage before him.

Sharing in Ghibli fandom is a practice commonly led online, in isolation; and when lucky, it's occasionally offline, at a cinema, with a few hundred others, tops. To be able to meet with so many others of the same parish (and with so many adorned in their ceremonial No-Face face paint) was an almost overwhelming reminder of the scale of the studio's, and Hisaishi's, power. This was a crowd ranging from die-hard, decades-long

Below: The orchestra plays the instruments, Joe plays the orchestra. Hisaishi in action conducting.

Overleaf: You've never heard *Totoro* like this. Hisaishi's concerts give the music of the forest spirit an almighty sound.

devotees to screeching children clad in *Totoro* onesies, and all the generations of Ghibli lovers in between, coming together in commune and in celebration. This show was in London, but this concert and this level of passionate crowd appeared across the world.

Beginning at the beginning, with the pulsing *Nausicaä of the Valley of the Wind* (1984), Hisaishi's set then ping-pongs through the Miyazaki filmography, his orchestra perfectly in sync to the Ghibli highlight reels playing on ginormous screens behind the orchestra. Rather than individual tracks, films have their own suites, condensing the breadth of the scores into concentrated waves of rolling joy. Tears and whoops cascade around the arena as this form enables Hisaishi to show off both the ingenuity and playfulness of his work: *Howl's Moving Castle* (2004) energetically darts around the orchestra to balance its tonal tight rope walk, while *Laputa: Castle in the Sky* (1986) positions brass players in the heights of the arena (like Pazu and his trumpet in the film) and *My Neighbour Totoro* (1988) takes the roof off, as a

40-strong choir add an almighty, almost comic, heft to its familiar "Totoro to-to-ro".

It's in the encore that the concert's emotional high point arrives, however. Months before the film would play to international audiences, Hisaishi performed the devastating 'Ask Me Why' from *The Boy and the Heron*. Isolated on the piano, the visibly nervous Hisaishi had the spotlight entirely on him for a whole song, for the first and only time that evening. Over the evening this enormous audience had shared an exuberant, exhaustive conversation with the composer, but here, tearful but beaming with pride and his hands quivering, he seemed to be talking to his old friend Miyazaki, using their own language of music and film which has crafted such unique beauty. It is a shame that Isao Takahata's *The Tale of the Princess Kaguya* (2013), which provoked one of Hisaishi's greatest scores, doesn't get a look-in, but perhaps that's for the next concert series – after all, he missed a few years, surely he has to come back soon?

Joe Outside Ghibli

While Joe Hisaishi is popularly known for his many collaborations with Hayao Miyazaki, he is a prolific artist with dozens of soundtracks and other projects to his name as composer, performer, arranger and conductor. His longstanding partnership with Takeshi Kitano (aka Beat Takeshi) saw him score eight of the Japanese auteur's films across a decade, including *A Scene at the Sea* (1991), *Sonatine* (1993), *Hana-bi* (1997) and *Kikujiro* (1999), all of which netted Joe prizes from the Japanese Academy.

And that's just the tip of the iceberg. Joe's film music discography comprises close to a hundred soundtrack albums, with highlights including his score for Yōjirō Takita's 2008 drama *Departures* and, naturally, countless anime soundtracks, ranging from the spectacular *Children of the Sea* (2019) to deeper cuts from the 1980s such as *Venus Wars* (1989), *Robot Carnival* (1987) and Arion (1986). He even directed his own film, *Quartet* (2001), a sensitively handled coming-of-age drama about, you guessed it, a string quartet, and he continues to conduct new recordings of canonical orchestral music by the likes of Stravinsky, Beethoven and Mahler.

But the real heads and crate diggers like to trace his musical journey back to the time before he became known first and foremost as a film score composer. Back then, Joe worked under a variety of aliases, crafting music that sat at the crossover between avant-garde jazz, minimalism, ambient soundscapes and hyper-melodic synth-pop. It's a heady mix, but intrepid travellers are advised to seek out MKWAJU Ensemble's *MKWAJU* (1981), Wonder City Orchestra's *Information* (1982), Manual Project's *Digital Fantasia* (1984) and Joe's own *Curved Music* (1986).

Ghibli Music Beyond Joe

**The best Ghibli film scores not created
by Joe Hisaishi.**

....

**The overture of a Joe Hisaishi score can transport people into a
Ghibli film before they've seen even a single frame of animation,
but he's not the only composer to lend their skills to the studio.**

Outside of Hayao Miyazaki's features (and one by Takahata), other artists, with different approaches ranging from big orchestral sound to intimate, singer-songwriter folk, have stamped their own mark on the aural history of the studio.

Isao Takahata never stuck with the same composer twice, which given his more iconoclastic approach to filmmaking, makes sense. None of his Ghibli films look the same, so none of them sound the same. Michio Mamiya's *Grave of the Fireflies* (1988) score

is haunting and beautiful, built around an innocent, tinkling synth line that sounds like a ghostly wind-up music box. In 1991, Katsu Hoshi's spacious piano lines became a perfect match for *Only Yesterday*'s drifts into nostalgia and memory. *Pom Poko*'s music, by band

Opposite: As well as a jukebox offering of 1960s tunes, *From Up On Poppy Hill* offers up a rambunctious score from Satoshi Takebe.

Below: Kyu Sakamoto, whose biggest track 'Ue o Muite Arukō' (or 'Sukiyaki') appears on the *From Up On Poppy Hill* track list.

Shang Shang Typhoon (member Manto Watanobe would also score *Ghiblies Episode 2* and short film *A Sumo Wrestler's Tail*), contrasts the 1994 film's inherent melancholy with tumbling, jingling instrumentation and simple, driving drums that befit the tanuki and their comical transformations and tummy-smacking joviality. Pop and jazz star Akiko Yano, a collaborator of Yellow Magic Orchestra, was then brought into the Ghibli fold in 1999 for *My Neighbours the Yamadas*, and stuck around to create the vocal-only scores for Miyazaki shorts *Looking for a Home* (2006) and *Mon Mon the Water Spider* (2006) as well as giving voice to Ponyo's sisters in 2008. It would be 14 years until Takahata's next score, when he turned to Joe Hisaishi.

In the mid-'90s to early '00s, the musical stylings of composer Yuji Nomi cropped up in a number of Ghibli projects. Having previously worked with mentor (and total legend) Ryuichi Sakamoto on the stunning 1987 anime feature *Royal Space Force: The Wings of*

Honnêamise (see our book *Anime Movie Guide* for a full chapter on that one), *Whisper of the Heart* (1995) saw Nomi pick up the conductor's baton for his first feature, creating a score that slaloms through the humdrum of suburbia and the glorious, regal realm of The Baron with gentle ease. From there came the scores for two Ghibli shorts, *Whale Hunt* (2001) and *Koro's Big Day Out* (2002), both directed by Hayao Miyazaki; then a return to feline pleasures, with *The Cat Returns* (2002), for a score that sways from playful, trilling pipes to wheezing *Sgt. Pepper* organs, balancing the film's light pleasures and strange psychedelia.

Later into the 2000s, with Ghibli experimenting with the development of the next generation of their directors, their productions brought in even more musical names. For 2006's *Tales From Earthsea*, composer Tamiya Terashima created sweeping orchestration, rivalling Howard Shore's work on the *Lord of the Rings* trilogy (2001–2003), to give the

film's stunning vistas real majesty; played alongside the various wind solos by multi-instrumentalist Carlos Núñez, which seem to reflect the film's heavy, personal dramas, there's a real sense of the epic and the intimate. For *Arrietty* (2010), French folk singer songwriter Cécile Corbel was flown in, marking the first time a score was made by a non-Japanese artist. A pan-European mixture, featuring among others Irish, Scottish and Turkish influences, the lyrical, plaintive soundtrack album would go on to sell over 200,000 copies.

Taking a big swing into swing, the music for Gorō Miyazaki's 2011 film *From Up on Poppy Hill* is a jazzier affair, from composer Satoshi Takebe. Full of the vigour of its characters, its boisterous grooves and slinking basslines occasionally give way to earned sentimentality, while still complementing various period songs from the film's '60s setting. Layered in hope and tragedy, Takatsugu Muramatsu's work for *When Marnie Was There* (2014) is one of the studio's most ambient works, gently shifting between calm

and anxiety, perfectly suited to the film's confused, adolescent heart. Following this, French composer Laurent Perez Del Mar joined the 2016 international co-production *The Red Turtle*, and provided huge waves of emotion, his swelling score saying what the near-silent characters don't. After a brief pause in activity for the studio, the sound of production soon restarted in the Ghibli office, and first out of the gate was *Earwig and the Witch* in 2020; it's a film that leaves much to be desired, but its score is a genuine highlight. Gorō Miyazaki returned to Satoshi Takebe, this time to create a headbanging delight, full of crashing drums, squealing organs and shredding guitars. Entirely glam, and entirely different to anything in the Ghibli music library, it's perhaps the film's biggest success.

Opposite (above): Cécile Corbel's music for *Arrietty* is beautiful and the film's soundtrack album became a commercial success.
Above: Michaël Dudok de Wit (left) and Laurent Perez Del Mar (right), director and composer for *The Red Turtle*.

The Ghibli Jukebox

It's not always the score that scores

....

**The most joyous musical moments in Ghibli's films don't have
to come from an original composition.**

Although the idea of a bespoke piece of music
translating and heightening the animation's message
sounds like the most direct route to audiovisual
ascension, it's in the alchemy of bringing together new
animation with old music that occasionally helps the
studio find more powerful magic. The right choice of
song can instantly ground a moment to a time and
space, it can yearn with lyrics too painful for characters
to speak, it can define an icon's arrival and it can
signify the departure of another's.

In *Grave of the Fireflies* (1988) the tragedy of
being unmoored from home and from innocence by
the forces of war, is both off-set and emboldened

by the warmth of Amelita Galli-Curci's vocals in her
performance of 'Home Sweet Home', a track from 1823
opera *Clari, or the Maid of Milan*, composed by
Henry Bishop and written by John Howard Payne. The
wistful, romantic musicality is steeped in melancholy.
Played on a record by a family safely returned to
their home, the song drifts on the wind from a palatial
residence towards the remnants of Seita and Setsuko's

Opposite: For *The Wind Rises*, Hayao Miyazaki returned to Arai's
music, discovering a perfect song for his film's end credits.

Below: Kiki flying through the streets of Koriko. *Kiki's Delivery
Service* contains one of Ghibli's finest musical moments, thanks to
Yumi Arai.

ramshackle dwelling, the ghost of Setsuko dancing to its homesick refrains.

After Japan emerged from the wreckage of the war, the year 1964 saw a new era of development both locally and globally, exemplified by the Tokyo Olympics, seen advertised on posters in the background of 2011's *From Up on Poppy Hill*. Featuring Ghibli's strongest playlist (and a delightfully breezy jazz score) this sophomore film by Gorō Miyazaki contains a pop classic that perfectly reflects the changing international sociopolitics of the time: Kyu Sakamoto's 'Ue o Muite Arukō', better known as 'Sukiyaki'. It was a hit in Japan, but perhaps more impressively, also marked the first time the US Billboard chart was topped by a song not in a European language.

J-pop icon Yumi Matsutoya provides two of Ghibli's most satisfying, poetically entwined needle drops, the first in 1989's *Kiki's Delivery Service* and the second, 24 years later, in *The Wind Rises*. Released under her birth name Yumi Arai, the first is played when Kiki flies off from home into the world of work. 'Rūju no Dengon', a mid-'70s riff on early '60s Americana pop rock, which plays on the portable radio that Kiki swings over her broom to help her surf the clouds into her new life. In 2013 Hayao Miyazaki returned to the artist, while on

the brink of his own retirement from professional life, in search of the ideal song for his film's end credits (and at the time, the curtain call on a career). For his film about a plane designer, Miyazaki chose the plaintive organs of 'Hikō-ki Gumo', a title translated as 'Vapour Trails', finding a perfect bookend for a character and for himself, circling back at the end of a career to the artist who had so perfectly accompanied the beginnings of youthful endeavour.

It's another American twist that provides perhaps the most joyous musical moment in any Ghibli film. 'Take Me Home, Country Roads', made famous by John Denver, is a song that feels so nostalgically bound to West Virginia, but in Yoshifumi Kondō's *Whisper of the Heart* (1995), the Tokyo suburb of Tama New Town claims the melody for its own. Although the film begins with Olivia Newton-John's cover of the song, it's another reversion (from composer Yuji Nomi), heartily performed by protagonist Shizuku, her violin-carving beau Seiji and a backing band of elderly men, that steals the show. Renamed 'Concrete Roads' to fit her suburban setting, the song has since become so wedded to the area that the unmistakable tune plays when you alight at Tama's Seiseki-sakuragaoka Station – it's almost heaven.

Jake's Ghibli Mix Tape

Top tunes from across the Ghibliverse

This is by no means our Top 10 Ghibli songs (maybe if we had a hundred spots, we could attempt that), but if you ever need an escape, this playlist should quickly transport you through Ghibli's grandest adventures and miniature masterpieces – via some undeniably catchy pop classics and devastating balladry. Cue them up for a quick sonic flight across treetops, wave crests and clubhouses, and then go and listen to all the other amazing music that's come out of the studio!

'The Path of the Wind'
Joe Hisaishi
My Neighbour Totoro (1988)

A celestial synth-laden dream and the heart of one of Hisaishi's greatest achievements. Makes the synthetic spiritual and the spiritual simple.

'Rūju no Dengon' (from the 1975 album *Cobalt Hour*)
Yumi Arai
Kiki's Delivery Service (1989)

You might not know what the words mean, but the unstoppable, unbridled and infectious joy in this track means it won't matter a bit.

'Take Me Home, Country Roads'
(originally by John Denver)
Yuji Nomi
Whisper of the Heart (1995)

Weighted more with hope than nostalgia, this wise remix of the classic emphasizes the collective idea of home, not just West Virginia.

'The Legend of Ashitaka'
Joe Hisaishi
Princess Mononoke (1997)

Hisaishi at his biggest and best. Beautiful, thunderous and mournful, a perfectly complex concentration of Miyazaki's war-faring world view.

'Ponyo on the Cliff by the Sea'
(2023 Symphonic Celebration version)
Joe Hisaishi
Ponyo (2008)

An enormous choir singing "Ponyo, Ponyo, Ponyo, fishy in the sea. Tiny little fishy, who could you really be?". Tidal waves of dopamine.

'Arrietty's Song'
Cécile Corbel
Arrietty (2010)

Contrasting Arrietty's small world with the ginormous outside, Corbel turns the small steps of plucked strings into a stirring, swirling baroque epic.

'Ue o Muite Arukō' (also known as 'Sukiyaki')
Kyu Sakamoto
From Up on Poppy Hill (2011)

It's been in *Mad Men*, Paul Thomas Anderson's *Inherent Vice* and it was even sent into space to the Gemini VII astronauts. An out-of-this-world bop.

'When I Remember This Life'
Kazumi Nikaido
The Tale of the Princess Kaguya (2013)

This extraordinary song grows from lilting lullaby to soulful paean for life, and its construction is captured in documentary *Isao Takahata and His Tale of the Princess Kaguya* (2013).

'Fine On the Outside'
Priscilla Ahn
When Marnie Was There (2014)

There's a lyrical directness here, exploring angst, isolation and inner strength, that brings quiet protagonist Anna's thoughts to musical life. Sombre but affirming stuff.

'Ask Me Why (Mahito's Commitment)'
Joe Hisaishi
The Boy and the Heron (2023)

Light in touch, but carrying hefty emotional and contextual weight, this short Hisaishi track lingers longer in the head and heart than most.

BONUS TRACK

'On Your Mark'
Chage and Aska
On Your Mark (1995)

This song is best known for having Hayao Miyazaki direct its music video, but even without the visuals this is still a very enjoyable, very sincere '90s power ballad.

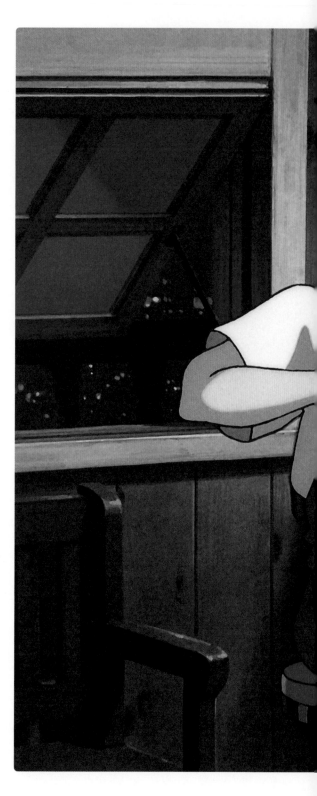

Previous page: He's big, furry and isn't too bad with an ocarina. Whether it's the film's score or the character itself, Totoro inspires great music.

Right: 'Take Me Home, Country Roads' may have appeared in *Kingsman: The Golden Circle*, *Alien: Covenant* and *Logan Lucky* but it's at its best in *Whisper of the Heart*.

4

Ghibli in Real Life

It makes sense that the studio that excels at finding the magic in the everyday would also find a way to leap off the screen and into our lives.

From theme parks to museums, stage productions to sweet cream puffs, there are so many ways to experience the world of Studio Ghibli. And yet, the studio has always ventured into these other spheres on its own terms. Of course, there are mountains of merchandise, but there's also a keen interest in craft, care and attention to detail. They are all works of art in their own right. Most importantly, these projects – which from a Western perspective are essentially brand exercises that exploit valuable intellectual property – are infused with the ingenuity and curiosity that epitomize Ghibli's work on screen: exposing fans young and old to galaxies of creation and expression that lie beyond the fringes of the Ghibliverse.

Ghibli Museum

If the Ghibliverse has a centre, the Ghibli Museum is it. Nestled in Inokashira Park in Mitaka, Western Tokyo – a regular haunt of Hayao Miyazaki when he was a youth – the Ghibli Museum is a place of wonder. A space of learning and inspiration that embraces a world of creativity, and which has been crafted like a Ghibli film in its own right.

It's to Miyazaki's credit that, when the opportunity arose following the release of *Princess Mononoke* (1997) to create a single location that could act as a magnet for Ghibli pilgrims from Japan and abroad, he approached the project with such vision and ambition. Far from a simple merchandise megastore, or a cynical excuse to bolster brand attachment, the Museum was conceived almost as its own original production, with a goal to delight and inspire like the greatest Ghibli adventure. Interest in *Totoro* and other Ghibli films may fade, Miyazaki thought, so for this project he had to dream bigger.

And so, as with many Ghibli films, everything stemmed from a proposal document penned by Miyazaki himself, called "This is the Kind of Museum I Want to Make!". In it he laid out the principles and aims for this unique museum in poetic stanzas, such as:

- A museum that is interesting and which relaxes the soul.

- A museum where much can be discovered.

- A museum based on a clear and consistent philosophy.

- A museum where those seeking enjoyment can enjoy, those seeking to ponder can ponder, and those seeking to feel can feel.

- A museum that makes you feel more enriched when you leave than when you entered!

Alongside this manifesto, Miyazaki created scores of image boards and design sketches for the Museum, ranging from bird's-eye-view drawings of the building itself to individual layouts of each room and exhibit, all the way down to the tiniest details – ceiling frescos, signage, light fixtures, even custom food flags for

the sandwiches sold in the Museum café. It was an outpouring of the imagination to rival *Spirited Away* (2001), which Miyazaki was developing at the same time. The director's dream for the Museum was for visitors to feel, much like Chihiro, that they were

Above: All aboard. It might not be on a Catbus, but *Totoro*-styled signage at least signals the way to the Ghibli Museum.

Opposite: The Ghibli Museum is full of stunning details, including a variety of striking stained glass artworks.

"entering a different world". Then, it fell to his son, Gorō Miyazaki, to oversee the actual building of the museum, and later serve as the Museum's director from its opening in October 2001.

Go to the Museum today and it is a magical, overwhelming experience. They don't make it awfully easy to get your tickets – thanks to an arcane booking system, with daily allocations released in batches, international pilgrims often have to set their alarm clocks for the wee small hours so they're ready to pounce once they go on sale. However, once you arrive at Inokashira Park, you are greeted by a building that is strange and beguiling by design. Its colourful central structure is made to look like it has been shaped out of children's modelling clay, while its roof is shrouded in greenery, and topped by a watchful, 5m (16ft) tall robot guardian from *Laputa: Castle in the Sky*. And who's that manning the ticket office? Why, it's Totoro himself.

However, while there are certain nods and references to Ghibli's films and iconic characters within the Museum itself – the largest of which is a giant cuddly Catbus that kids (and *only* kids) are allowed to climb – the exhibits and world of the Museum itself are remarkably ingenious and unfamiliar. The Museum's slogan is *Let's get lost, together!* and throughout the whole building there is a sense of free-form discovery, with little nooks and crannies, tiny details and secret passageways that are custom-made for the infinite curiosity of the childlike mind. Isao Takahata, who

Above: Tap Cat. Miyazaki and the designers poured everything into the tiniest details of the Museum.

Right: The exterior of the Ghibli Museum in Mitaka, Tokyo, looking as strange and inviting as one of Ghibli's films.

didn't play a role in the making of the Museum, put it best in an essay reflecting on his first visit. "At a theme park like Disneyland for example," he wrote, "you sit in the attraction's seat and let the rides excite and dizzy you like a Miyazaki animation does. It is easy and effortless, but totally passive. Yet in a museum, you must take an active part in the experience. Here at the Museum, the children and adults are the ones playing the storytelling roles of the movie characters."

So, where will your story take you? Perhaps you'll start with one of the permanent exhibitions, which are showcases of the history and craft of the art of animation. On the ground floor, you can find zoetropes and other physical contraptions that make the magic trick of animation three-dimensional and tactile, while upstairs is a five-room walkthrough experience called "Where a Film is Born", which traces the production process from sketch to finished animation across a series of densely detailed, mock workshops filled with research materials, paint and pencils and artwork – even paintings by Miyazaki himself from his student days.

The first of these rooms is sometimes referred to as "A Boy's Room – A Gift from Grampa", hinting at Miyazaki's intention of welcoming youngsters into the bustle and clutter of an idealized artist's study, as if they've inherited it, and that sense of inheritance is at the heart of the whole Ghibli Museum project. In the weighty tome *Hayao Miyazaki and the Ghibli Museum*, which was published in 2019, Museum Managing Director Kazuki Anzai remarks that Miyazaki believes that he and the team behind the Museum are "the bearers of popular culture". "As [Miyazaki] created a museum and engaged in making exhibit objects," Anzai writes, "he came to realize that the popular culture that we are bearing is being continuously inherited by people here and there around the world... He also says that the baton handed to us in the relay race that we are

Opposite: A giant statue of the caretaker robot from *Laputa: Castle in the Sky* stands on top of the Ghibli Museum

Below: The Ghibli Museum pulls back the curtain on the creative process, with sketches, paintings and artwork on display to inspire.

running is one that we will hand off to the next set of runners."

The Ghibli Museum was built from the ground up as a direct dialogue with the impressionable, imaginative young mind. We've written at length elsewhere in this book about the short films that Studio Ghibli has produced exclusively for the Museum (see Chapter 2: Ghibli Deep Cuts), but the venue for these screenings, the Saturn Theater, was planned by Miyazaki as a welcoming and impactful cinema experience for small visitors. He paid great attention to everything from the lighting of the room (so as not to frighten kids afraid of the dark), to the dimensions of the bench-type seating, to the design of the projection booth – all with the goal of giving kids an exciting and inspiring opportunity to watch animation on the big screen.

For the "MAMMA AIUTO!" gift shop, which is stuffed with delightful Ghibli merchandise and other oddities, Miyazaki put together a set of paints that he himself uses, with an illustrated guide that instructs newcomers how to get the best out of it. Elsewhere, the "Tri Hawks" reading room is lined with bookshelves: one side is filled with art books, storyboard collections and other insightful deep dives into the art behind Ghibli's

films; while the other is a library of children's classics, stocked with books personally picked by Miyazaki and Museum curators. Scan the shelves and you'll find works that Ghibli has adapted into feature films, but you're more likely to have your horizons broadened by carefully selected gems from the shared cultural heritage of world literature.

This is what sets the Ghibli Museum apart from Walt Disney's Disneyland and Disney World projects. Where Disney's Parks have become an exercise in recreating the excitement of a beloved film or franchise (or vigilantly maintained intellectual property), the Ghibli Museum looks out into the cosmos of creative

Above: The peculiar colour of the Museum's exterior is intended to resemble children's modelling clay.

Opposite: "Attention to detail leads to the whole". Several wonderful details from inside the Ghibli Museum, including a wall painting that evokes Kiki's hometown of Koriko (far left), a sign pointing the way to the Saturn Theater cinema (top), the crest of the Museum itself (middle), with pictures of three hawks and boars' heads (puns on the Japanese for Mitaka and Inokashira), and the sublime ceiling fresco, with plants painted by veteran art director Kazuo Oga (bottom).

endeavour: rather than a space for promotion, it's a space for curation.

That's perhaps no better seen than in the Museum's programme of special exhibitions, which are housed in a two-room space across from the workshop area. These have ranged from in-depth insights into the production of pre-Ghibli masterworks such as *Heidi, Girl of the Alps* and *Future Boy Conan* to celebrations of the work of specific filmmakers that share a kinship with Ghibli, such as Russian animator Yuri Norstein and British stop-motion maestros Aardman Animations.

Some, though, are more essayistic in concept. Exhibitions on the folktale *Goldilocks and the Three Bears* and E. T. A. Hoffmann's festive fairy tale *The Nutcracker and the Mouse King* both interrogated the enduring impact of those stories on generations of children, using illustrations, manga, image boards and three-dimensional exhibition objects to bring the stories to life – gigantic bear models for the former, and an intricate "Noisy Theatrical" diorama for the latter.

And then there are those exhibitions that are conceived as investigations into the interconnectedness of popular culture, and Miyazaki's part within that web of influence and inspiration. "The Gift of Illustrations" showcased fairy tale artwork from Andrew Lang's *Fairy Books*, and "The Haunted Tower" used short stories by Robert Westall and Edogawa Ranpo as a springboard for an exploration of the clock tower as a device in storytelling, encompassing everything from novelists Wilkie Collins, Arthur Conan Doyle and Maurice Leblanc to Miyazaki's own Lupin III feature, *The Castle of Cagliostro* (1979).

Toshio Suzuki says that it was his idea for the Museum's tickets to consist of a series of frames snipped from a Ghibli film – although, if you dig through Miyazaki's many image boards, you'll find rough sketches of young visitors, holding up their ticket to the light, gazing at the images within. Whoever came up with it, though, it nevertheless provides an apt way of viewing the Museum as a whole: it invites us to look through Studio Ghibli's films and discover a whole enthralling universe beyond them.

Top: All (children) aboard! The Catbus provides a kids-only spot for play at the Ghibli Museum.

Right: Full of hidden delights and secret passages built especially for children, the Museum encourages exploration.

Ni-Tele Really Big Clock

Nittere Ōdokei

Jutting out of the headquarters of Nippon Television in Shiodome, Tokyo, this enormous, copper, chicken-legged, time-keeping castle was designed by Hayao Miyazaki.

Opened in 2006, the steampunk sculpture, appearing to be made up of interconnected metal rooms adorned with cannon-covered turrets, mushroom-shaped roofing and even clawed feet clearly shared an architect with Howl. Arrive at the right time of day, like many Ghibli fans do, and this castle starts to move too.

As the hour is struck (selected times may vary), lantern-headed metal men dotted around the structure shake into clockwork action, starting to crank and hammer away like blacksmiths, perhaps making something or perhaps just keeping this clock ticking. Emblematic of Miyazaki's ongoing mechanical fascination – as seen in the huge, detailed airships of *Nausicaä of the Valley of the Wind* (1984) or the

workshops of *Porco Rosso* (1992) – the scene begins. Waltzing music starts, secret doors open, cogs turn and lights spin and for a few minutes the sharp edges of a modern metropolitan district are forgotten, as a bizarre and beautiful giant automaton from one of the world's greatest artists chugs through a captivating metallic dance, one that seems to be celebrating the craft of building its own stage. Then time's up! Just as quickly as it started, it's over and the Ghibli pilgrims disperse, beaming at seeing one of their favourite directors showing his creativity in such a different form – time.

Below: Although hidden between sleek office buildings, the Really Big Clock has become an essential discovery for Ghibli fans.

Shirohige's Cream Puff Factory

A Taste of Totoro

The film *My Neighbour Totoro* (1988) established the now iconic
character that adorns Ghibli's logo, and in the decades since Totoro's
debut, fans have been able to experience their beloved character
in various experiential ways outside of the sights and sounds of its
original cinematic form.

Plush toys let you *feel* Totoro, the Ghibli Park's Dondoko
Forest lets you *inside* Totoro, but at Shirohige's Cream
Puff Factory in Daita, Western Tokyo (and at a second
location in Kichijoji, much nearer the Ghibli Museum, if
you're making plans), you can *taste* Totoro.

Officially endorsed by the studio (and reportedly run
by one of Miyazaki's relatives), the Cream Puff Factory
is, like in a Ghibli adventure, a revelation tucked behind
a winding series of mundane streets. Adorned with a
humble, easily missed sign, the factory – which is really
just a café – sits on a greenery-covered street corner and
inside you'll find two floors of Ghibli fans, huddled around
tables, chomping into one of their favourite characters.

Made from exceptional choux pastry, shaped into
a round base, with two simplified pastry-prong ears

and a pair of bright, wide fondant eyes, these Totoro
treats are almost too cute to eat – almost. Filled with a
rotating variety of flavours (on our last visit chocolate,
hazelnut, vanilla and strawberry cheesecake were the
orders of the day), the puffs are light, flaky and moreish.
And they do also reflect the nature of the character
they're based on, not just because of their shape but
because they are enormously sweet. With its sense of
everyday magic and its clear focus on craft, Shirohige's
Cream Puff Factory is a must for any Ghibli fan,
especially a hungry one.

Above: My Neighbour Profiterole. The handsomely styled cream
puffs emerge from the factory sporting appropriate headwear.

Ghibli Park

The ultimate destination for any Ghibli fan

Making fantasy a reality – the magic trick that Ghibli films so often pull on us. One second a girl is roaming through empty streets, streets just like ones we know, and then suddenly, after making the right turn at the right place, she steps into the mythical Cat Kingdom.

Whether it is down an alley, through a tunnel, or within a crumbling tower, other worlds are hiding within our own, and these films help us discover them.

Making reality a fantasy – that's the next trick. The one that's even harder. If you transport a viewer into another world, you can surprise them with things they've never seen, delighting them with dazzling design. But through Ghibli's eye for detail, through the power of imagination – theirs and their characters' – our own lives can become charmed by their magical redecoration. Like when Lisa reveals two simple bowls of instant ramen, to her cold, wet, doting young audience in *Ponyo*. The hearty noodles, hunks of ham and glistening fat appear

like the welcome resurrection at the end of a disappearing act, emerging from a puff of steam – abracadabra indeed.

Despite their transportive effect, those tricks have always existed within the confines of the viewing experience, until the creation of the Ghibli Park. This is definitively not a theme park; there are no roller coasters, carousels or stunt shows here. Instead this is

Below: The central steps of Ghibli's Grand Warehouse. Look closely and you might see the mosaic tiles hiding some familiar characters.

a slighter, leisurely paced adventure that actualizes the dream of so many fans: to step inside a Ghibli film.

Having created a universally beloved Ghibli Museum, Gorō Miyazaki, the former landscape architect, was once again handed the reins to bring the studio into this new reality. Rather than a sprawling, Disney-esque plan to build an entire town that could reshape entertainment as we know it, the beginnings of the Ghibli Park are fairly humble. "Would you like to repurpose a facility that used to be a heated pool and create an exhibition facility with a storage function?" the Aichi Prefecture asked Ghibli, at which point Gorō knew "the story of Ghibli Park [had] begun". Built within the 460 acres of the Expo 2005 Aichi Commemorative Park (the location of a large "world's fair" event), the park contains five key areas: The Valley of the Witches, which features a recreation of the bakery from *Kiki's Delivery Service* (1989) and a towering version of Howl's castle; Mononoke Village, a learning centre, styled like the wooden fortress from the titular film;

Dondoko Forest, which contains a full-size version of Satsuki and Mei's house (originally built for the 2005 expo) and a large Totoro-shaped climbing frame; the Hill of Youth, featuring the park's Jules Verne-styled clock-tower entrance, as well as locations inspired by *Whisper of the Heart* (1995) and *The Cat Returns* (2002), including the central antique shop; and Ghibli's Grand Warehouse, the glorious centrepiece, built on the old swimming pool.

Interlinking all of the areas are perfect rolling hills (you can almost see Kiki resting on them), vibrant flower beds, forests cooing with life, and the feverish, wonderful sound of excitable children – and equally excited grown-ups. If you've been lucky enough to secure a ticket for every area, you'll follow pathways

Above: The Ghibliotheque gang (from left to right: Jake, producer Steph and Michael) join No-Face for a photo-op at Ghibli Park.

Opposite: Hidden within the Dondoko Forest section of the Park is Dondoko-do, a Totoro-shaped structure built for climbing.

through the park, and along the way encounter benches that feature a bronze statue of a familiar character (like Muta the cat or Mr Yamada) or the belongings of a character who's just run off (like Mei's hat and sweetcorn or Shun's satchel from *From Up on Poppy Hill*). These are one of many Easter eggs in the park, perfect for the curious, or obsessive, fan to discover as they roam.

When exploring the park, architectural historian Terunobu Fujimori was immediately struck by the sense of diversity and timelessness carried by the structures, which, as they are recreations of structures from the films, reflects similarly on those too. In a publication

created for the park, he explains that the buildings have "characteristics of unknown nationality, both inside and outside, not converging on any country or period" and that "in another 100 years, ordinary people may be telling the urban legend that time is reversed, that Mr. Miyazaki came up with the story of Totoro when he happened to see [Mei and Satsuki's] house while taking a walk." Who knows then what ideas will be conjured in the imagination of the kids exploring it now, as they step into their favourite stories, hearing the "thumping sound of violins being made" or bending "down to look through a window" and seeing "a large white cat stretching out ... looking at [you] with a bold look in its eyes".

Considering the Park's potential construction, Toshio Suzuki said he was "desperately hoping for it in [his] heart", both for him, and as a means of continuing the legacy of Ghibli. Although derided by some fans for his films, Suzuki is sincere in his admiration for Gorō: "The day when Miya-san and I retire is coming soon, but the spirit of Ghibli will be carried on by Gorō. That's obvious when you look at this park." Knowing how much of a perfectionist his father is, and how much of a keen eye Suzuki has had on all aspects of Ghibli's output for decades, it's perhaps surprising to learn that "Gorō didn't consult Miya-san or me about anything when creating this park". Worrying? Not at all. "Ghibli is imbued in every detail of the park. That's what Gorō did."

But how do you find the essence of something that lives on a screen? It's a challenge not lost on Gorō. He says: "we often hear the phrase 'Ghibli-like' but when we ask people, 'What do you think "Ghibli-like" means?', a surprisingly large number of people are at a loss for an answer. I think it's because Studio Ghibli works seem to have a sense of unity, but in reality, they don't. The location, era and style vary depending on the work and director." It's Ghibli's Grand Warehouse, the glorious main attraction of the Park, that may be Gorō's crowning achievement for the studio, because here he finds that unity in the differences, realizing the feeling of Ghibli's collective work – and doing so using an old swimming pool.

Above: The clock tower that welcomes visitors hides an elevator. Pilgrims descend from the real world and emerge in Ghibli Park.

Left: It's not just the buildings in the Grand Warehouse that are a patchwork, the Catbus is too.

Upon entering, the visitor turns a corner and stares up at a huge, glass palace (not unlike London's crystal one, which held its own world expo in 1851). It's filled with a patchwork of buildings, painted and styled very differently, all tied together by a stunning mosaic staircase ("as impressive as the Grand Staircase of the Piazza di Spagna in Rome," notes Fujimori). With water spilling down its sides, feeding plants at its base, the mosaic ties the space back to its original form as a pool while guiding visitors into new delights. "Ghibli's Great Warehouse is a mess," Gorō says. "There are no maps posted, and no signs showing the route", but spend enough hours in there and you may encounter, among so much else: Yubaba's bathhouse office; a full-size robot from *Laputa: Castle in the Sky* (1986); a scaled-up version of Arrietty's tiny world; a walk-through archive of Ghibli Museum exhibits; a kids-only area filled with characters to clamber over and in; an exhibition of Ghibli artwork and merchandise, both Japanese and international; a restaurant inspired by *Porco Rosso* (1992); a cinema playing Ghibli shorts; a rotating special exhibition – for our visit, we were lucky enough for it to be about Ghibli food; and a gloriously silly opportunity to step inside life-size dioramas of iconic moments from the films. (Yes, sitting on the train with No-Face is fun, but getting punched in the face by Porco? That's a knockout.) Oh, and the gift shop of course. Make sure you leave a lot of space in your suitcase to make the most out of it.

The history of the studio is celebrated in great detail in the exhibitions, which for older visitors is fascinating, but is not dissimilar to the Ghibli Museum. Where the Park provides the most joy is in the alleyways from *Spirited Away* (2001), the cluttered rooms of the *From Up on Poppy Hill* (2011) clubhouse and the enormous plant pots and water droplets from *Arrietty* (2010) – these are where fans young and old can experience the uncanny pleasure of entering the worlds they've previously only clamoured for in 2D. It's perhaps in the reactions of visitors that the Park reveals its greatest power. Here, the faces of others, whatever their generation, light up at the sight of a statue, a storefront or even an ice cream, knowing they can finally touch and taste through their screens. But it's more than a composite of a fictitious moment; it becomes something new in the mind of the traveller, born from the structure of one story but now untethered to be part of limitless others. Is this what Gorō was tasked with chasing? Not emulation but creation? In taking the puzzle pieces of all of Ghibli's works, he did not produce an homage to them, but rather assembled them to create a new work in itself. One that can translate into as much joy as any of the films.

At the end of Terunobu Fujimori's trip to the warehouse, he stared out from a high balcony at the maze of creation below him, where the tiles of the patchwork disappear and the whole, new artwork comes into view. He thought, "When I look at Ghibli's streets, I feel like my body is floating in a mixture of reality and unreality, and I want to stare at them forever." Magic.

Above: Toshio Suzuki, the puppeteer behind so many Ghibli ventures, alongside the official artwork for the Ghibli Park.

Spirited Away

Live on stage

....

Whether by design or by chance, in the years following the COVID-19 pandemic, Studio Ghibli became more visible than ever — including, most notably, in the world of theatre.

Perfectly timed to the run-up to the release of *The Boy and the Heron* (2023), two large-scale productions of Hayao Miyazaki's most beloved films, *My Neighbour Totoro* (1988) and *Spirited Away* (2001), were brought to the stage within months of each other in 2022, to great success and international acclaim.

Spirited Away was first out of the gate. It was first unveiled in 2021 as an upcoming production by Toho for its Imperial Theater in Tokyo, a grand auditorium that seats 1,900 spectators. Tony and Olivier Award-winning director John Caird, who had brought productions such as *Les Misérables* and *Candide* to the Imperial Theater in the past, had proposed *Spirited Away* as a potential project after dreaming of filling

the massive theatre with something "authentically" Japanese. As he told Megan Peters at Comicbook.com, he asked himself the question: "What might be the great big Japanese story that would appeal to a big audience?" His thoughts almost immediately turned to "the greatest Japanese storyteller alive today": Hayao Miyazaki.

Caird met with Toshio Suzuki to secure Ghibli's permission, and was surprised when Miyazaki himself

Opposite: This adaptation featured two rotating casts, including Kanna Hashimoto and Mone Kamishiraishi as Chihiro.

Below: From Screen to Stage. Director John Caird and his team had the task of bringing *Spirited Away* into the real world.

BASED ON THE ANIMATED FEATURE FILM BY HAYAO MIYAZAKI

SPIRITED AWAY
Live on Stage

ADAPTED BY **JOHN CAIRD** CO-ADAPTED BY **MAOKO IMAI**

ORIGINAL SCORE BY JOE HISAISHI MUSIC SUPERVISION, ORCHESTRATIONS AND ARRANGEMENTS BY BRAD HAAK ASSOCIATE MUSIC SUPERVISION, ORCHESTRATIONS, AND ABLETON PROGRAMMING BY CONOR KEELAN

SET DESIGNER JON BAUSOR PUPPETRY DESIGN AND DIRECTION TOBY OLIÉ

CHOREOGRAPHER / STAGING SHIGEHIRO IDE LIGHTING DESIGNER JIRO KATSUSHIBA SOUND DESIGNER KOICHI YAMAMOTO COSTUME DESIGNER SACHIKO NAKAHARA HAIR AND MAKE UP DESIGNER HIROAKI MIYAUCHI PROJECTION DESIGNER SATOSHI KURIYAMA

MUSIC DIRECTOR / CONDUCTOR ERIKA FUKASAWA STAGE MANAGER TAKASHI HOJO ASSISTANT TO THE DIRECTOR MAOKO IMAI ASSISTANT DIRECTORS MAKOTO NAGAI / RYUSEI ONUKI PRODUCER HARUKA OGI

DIRECTED BY **JOHN CAIRD**

IN ASSOCIATION WITH STUDIO GHIBLI PRESENTED BY TOHO CO., LTD.

joined them for the meeting. "We had a lovely hour together, chatting about the play and how it would work and what I imagined it to be like," Caird told Daniel Dockery at Crunchyroll. "[Miyazaki] was so interesting, just talking with Toshio Suzuki about their memories of creating the film and what inspired them to make changes in the process."

Suzuki and Miyazaki had both been impressed by Caird's vision for the production. For all its imagination (and dozens of divine creatures), *Spirited Away* is essentially set around one key location: the bathhouse. That would give the show the chance to be epic and beautiful, but still contained and achievable within a theatre setting. "If you can find a way to put a bathhouse on stage," Caird argued, "then you've solved 90 per cent of the story."

With Ghibli on board, Caird gathered his key collaborators, including puppet designer Toby Olié, who had worked on the National Theatre's blockbuster 2007 production of *War Horse*, and set designer Jon Bausor, who had previously collaborated with Caird on the Imperial Theater production of *A Knight's Tale*, a Japanese-language musical that drew from Shakespeare and Chaucer. Working remotely due to pandemic-related travel restrictions, the team developed a take on *Spirited Away* which had all of the magic

of Miyazaki's original film but also the tactile, intimate quality of live theatre.

"Theatre magic isn't film magic," Caird explained to Slashfilm's Joshua Meyer. "You're not creating the impossible. You are creating something that's beautiful, and you're showing the audience how you're doing it. But it's still magic, even though they can see how it's done. It's a sort of conspiracy, if you like, between the performer and the audience to agree that something has reality on stage."

While closely hewing to the storyline and iconography of the film, with songs inserted from the accompanying Image Album soundtrack, the *Spirited Away* stage production had to evoke the scale and densely populated bustle of the central bathhouse location, while bringing some of Miyazaki's most unique and beguiling creations to life. Caird and co had a few theatrical tricks up their sleeve, including using an alternating cast, with leads Kanna Hashimoto and Mone Kamishiraishi (who voiced the female lead in Makoto Shinkai's *Your Name*) sharing the role of Chihiro between them – something that feeds into the theme of doubles and doppelgängers running throughout the story. Caird and Bausor were also inspired by various traditions of Japanese theatre and performance, from Noh to kabuki to sumo wrestling, in the staging and choreography of many of the

production's sequences. "The brilliant idea Jon had," Caird explained, "is that he's taken essentially a Noh theatre stage and put it in the middle of a Western stage, which was a wonderful way of bringing deep-seated Japanese culture into the proceedings."

Elsewhere, puppetry and performance combine to spellbinding effect. As the imposing witch Yubaba shifts emotional gears from the quietly sinister to the positively incandescent, alternating actresses Mari Natsuki and Romi Park (the former reprising her role from the original film) are swarmed by puppeteers holding individual, oversized facial features, merging to form one giant, furious Yubaba head. During the memorable scene where Chihiro is tasked with cleaning up a Stink Spirit that has wandered into the bathhouse, a transparent blanket of fabric covers actress and puppet-creation as imaginary water and suds rain down from above; then, a billowing roll of brown fabric flows across the stage as the mud and garbage lodged inside the Spirit are spewed across the whole bathhouse floor.

It's these simple ideas that make the most impression: when we are first introduced to the mysterious No-Face, the creature is performed by a single dancer, whose erratic movements give it an unnerving, unseemly quality. Later, when No-Face goes on its gluttonous rampage through the bathhouse, more

dancers are added underneath its shroud-like costume as it grows and grows into a gruesome monster, with a large set of puppeteered teeth exposed from its torso. "That was more fun for the audience and more fun for the performers," John Caird explained to Polygon. "It didn't rely on anything technical. It could just rely on the skill of the performance."

Spirited Away premiered in February 2022, running in Tokyo for two months before touring around the country, with legs in Osaka, Hakata and Sapporo, before closing in Nagoya in July. Later that year, a filmed performance of the play was made available to stream in Japan, and a release in North America followed in 2023, first on the big screen as part of distributor GKIDS' annual Studio Ghibli Fest programme, and then on home video. Fans outside of Japan and North America seethed with jealousy, but those within reach of the UK were consoled by the news that the production would transfer to the London stage for a limited season at the Coliseum Theatre from April 2024.

Opposite (above): Show-Face. These Ghibli stage productions are unafraid to make the puppeteers part of the action – and the magic.

Above: Dragon, Fly. Even though it is contained by the proscenium of a stage, *Spirited Away* doesn't skimp on spectacle.

My Neighbour Totoro

The story of the play

....

In the midst of the COVID-19 pandemic, while stuck at home, the writer Tom Morton-Smith told us that he was "having a hallucination that [he] was adapting *My Neighbour Totoro*" as a play.

Considering the fraught, confusing circumstances at the time, escaping from reality in such a way would've been more than acceptable – but this was reality. Morton-Smith, whose acclaimed plays had included stories about the creation of the atomic bomb and the launch of the Large Hadron Collider, was putting physics on the back burner (or off the bunsen burner) and replacing it with Ghibli.

A project spearheaded by composer (and here executive producer) Joe Hisaishi, working with the Royal Shakespeare Company, *My Neighbour Totoro* (1988) was going to become a play, launching at London's Barbican theatre and produced by live theatre innovators Improbable and Japan's Nippon TV. This was news both thrilling and confounding to fans of the studio. The prospect of seeing anything new

from the studio, especially something with the force of Joe Hisaishi behind it, was exciting – but how could it possibly work? In animation, anything is possible, and Ghibli are better than anyone at using the form's unreality, hidden in the illusory seams of filmmaking and viewing, to great power. On stage, though, once the curtain comes up, there's no hiding. Totoro, a giant furry, ocarina-playing forest spirit who can fly on a spinning top, *had* to come to life.

Phelim McDermott, director and co-founder and co-artistic director of theatre company Improbable,

Opposite: Super Group. The poster artwork for the *Totoro* stage show, showcasing the key creative partners, assembled under executive producer Joe Hisaishi.

Below: Totoro, or not Totoro? The challenge of adapting Miyazaki's classic fell to the Royal Shakespeare Company.

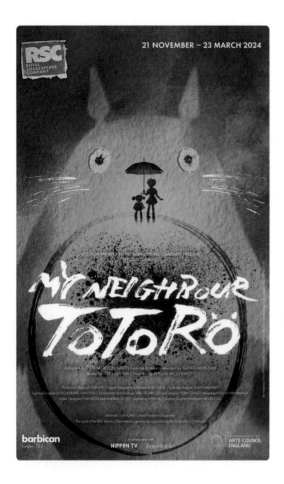

that are the heart of the film for him: "it's an exploration about kindness, about how people interact with each other", and for Satsuki and Mei "the fact their mum might die is the biggest, most epic feeling they could possibly have." In Miyazaki's hands the story contains weight, but is never heavy; it's wonderfully escapist yet grounded, welcoming us into a new fantasy world with such ease, it's hard to tell where the threshold was crossed. "When you're watching a play you just let the world of it kind of flow over you," the writer explains. "The closest I've ever got to that in the cinema is with *Totoro*."

Before the hallucinations at the desk, a visit to Ghibli was set up for the team. This is hallowed territory for any animation fan, and they were guided around the studio, discussing the production, with Toshio Suzuki ("he let me hold the Oscar for *Spirited Away*," Morton-Smith recounts) and eventually with Hayao Miyazaki himself. Separating himself from the production, or perhaps just keen to get back to making *The Boy and the Heron* (2023), Miyazaki made just two points: that the play needed to be "its own thing" in relation to the film, and that Totoro wasn't to be "just a fluffy man in a suit", and crucially could "be a bit smelly".

Having said yes to directing the show because his "children made him", McDermott now needed someone who could actually bring Totoro to life ("not my concern", jokes Morton-Smith). Getting humans on stage would be relatively easy, but how about something as huge as Totoro, and with such identifiable characteristics and movements? Someone who matched the optimistic "and yes" spirit of McDermott's improvisational practice was necessary. Enter puppeteer Basil Twist, a MacArthur "Genius Grant" winner. He believes "there is still nothing more magical than when a seemingly inanimate object comes to life before your eyes", but bringing Miyazaki's creatures to life couldn't be a one-man job. So Twist, who initially wanted to be an animator before getting hooked on puppetry via *The Muppets*, went straight to the source of his fascination: Jim Henson's Creature Shop. Inspired by the Japanese bunraku form of puppetry, in which the puppeteers are visible, Twist and the Henson team set about creating a variety of characters, some the size of a tennis ball, some the size of half the stage and always "thrilling and majestic, as it should be, when you discover a giant forest spirit".

who had been introduced to Hisaishi via mutual friend and legendary modern composer Philip Glass, was up for the task. "I love the challenge of staging something that's unstageable," he reveals in the show's programme, but he was initially clueless, saying to Joe Hisaishi: "we'll have to ask the spirits" how to do it. The sell-out first run would scoop up a whopping six Olivier awards – including Best Director and Best Entertainment or Comedy Play – so now we know that *Totoro* is perfectly stageable, but in 2018, the prospect was a riddle.

Prior to diving deep into Ghibli, Morton-Smith's Japanese cinema experiences had been shaped by the gnarly shocks of films like *Tetsuo: The Iron Man* (1989) and *Audition* (1999), but then came *Totoro*, a film that he would seek out whenever it played on a big screen. Though he is drawn to the story's invention and fantastical aspects, it's the humans and their feelings

Puppetry is "a very simple magic that's very profound", according to Twist. That's also a great way of describing the show in which his puppets appear. Staged around a rotatable, deconstructable version of the Kusakabe family home, the expansions in Morton-Smith's script (developed alongside the film's storyboards, as there was never an actual film script) keep fantasy in the fringes and focus on the humans that surround this home and developing their journeys. The treatment of Yasuko (Satsuki and Mei's mother) is explored in more detail, as is the relationship between their father Tatsuo and his wife. Surrounding villagers are expanded upon too, like the young boy Kanta, who evolves beyond awkwardness into a bit of a hapless romantic, or Granny, who reveals a tragic pain that could be shared by the Kusakabe family.

These familiar, and now widened, stories become enriched incredibly powerfully by their staging – and by the arrival of some remarkable creatures. Set behind the house, in the twisting branches of a forest, are a live band, who add a sense of immediacy and playful delight to Joe Hisaishi's magnificent score, their visible inclusion the first of many self-aware reveals of the play's own form. The Soot Sprites, showing the clearest instance of Twist's bunraku influence, are black tufts on the end of metre-long black fingers – or "Freddy Krueger gloves" to Morton-Smith – that are danced around the stage by a chorus of cast members. These cast members are the show's stage hands and vice versa, seen moving sets around and transforming into characters. Even small moments, like the arrival of a bus or a goat, are opportunities to show these Sprites and thus the play's artificiality, which only strengthens their meaning in reality. These are magical figures of nature, yet they are present, manipulating our experience and guiding characters towards hope and survival, and revealed by puppeteers who are, of course, human. In showing the workings, Twist takes an approach that underlines Ghibli's constant reinforcing of the relationship between human, nature and the supernatural, and how tight the domains and binds between each are.

Right: The Sprite Stuff. *Totoro's* team of ace puppeteers, bearing their "Freddy Krueger finger" Soot Sprite puppets.

Now, on to the elephant in the room – and he is about that size. Having spoken to many people during the interval of different performances of *My Neighbour Totoro*, we noticed that the thing people most often say first is: "He is massive!". And he is. He is absolutely huge. Basil Twist was in San Francisco, in his parents' house (his mother is a puppeteer) and on the other side of a pandemic-induced Zoom call when he began building, using bits of "plastic and fabric and cardboard" to pull off a miracle and bring Totoro to beautiful, enormous life. When Mei, played by an adult woman, climbs onto the belly of this slowly scratching, head-lolling kaiju-plushie, she looks the size of the toddler she's playing. It's an incredible thing to witness, and every moment featuring the creatures of the forest from there onwards becomes its own breathtaking, joyous dream. Sequences that seem so otherworldly, like Totoro's flight, the forest-growing Dondoko dance, the bus stop, *anything* with a Catbus in, they somehow all work within this version of reality, where this play has greeted us halfway, admitted its falseness and encouraged our own imagination to help meet it. For the adults in the audience, it's a hugely impressive artistic and experimental exercise in adaptation; for the children (and let's be honest, most of the adults), it's a

fantasy at arm's length – you can almost smell it. Now it's entered reality, can the magic of Miyazaki's story just keep going, keep growing? McDermott says: "The *Totoro* story will never stop. The totoro will last longer than human beings." So about as long as the show's standing ovation.

Top: A fan-favourite cameo in the original film, the stage production of *Totoro* brings the local village goat to vivid life.

Above: And the Olivier goes to... Tom Morton-Smith, Griselda Yorke, and Kenichi Yoda, receiving the Noël Coward Award for Best Entertainment or Comedy Play.

Opposite: Ensemble in the Sky. *Totoro's* innovative stage setting places the musicians high above the treetops.

Treading the Boards

The recent blockbuster productions of *Spirited Away* and *My Neighbour Totoro* may hog the limelight, but they're far from the first times that the work of Studio Ghibli has been brought to the stage. In 2013, Whole Hog Theatre's acclaimed take on *Princess Mononoke* sold out a run at London's New Diorama Theatre in mere hours, and moved to Japan for a highly successful Tokyo transfer. That latter leg of the production drew positive notices from none other than Miyazaki himself. Actress Mei Mac performed in the lead role, a decade before being cast as Mei in the *Totoro* show, and recalls the company visiting Studio Ghibli headquarters, where Miyazaki told her, "I've never imagined San as a real-life human being, but if she did exist, it would be you." Director Alexandra Rutter has continued to adapt Japanese animation for the stage, with the Whole Hog production of Makoto Shinkai's *Garden of Words* appearing in 2021. For a distinctly Japanese stage version of Miyazaki's work, seek out the kabuki theatre production of *Nausicaä of the Valley of the Wind*, which had a limited run at Tokyo's Shinbashi Enbujo Theatre in 2019, but has since been issued on Japanese Blu-ray.

5

Ghibli
Book Club

From the page to the
screen... and back again!

Studio Ghibli has long drawn inspiration from the work of the world's greatest children's authors, and has brought a good few of their books to the big screen, too – and, unlike other companies, they are happy to repay the favour and act as a gateway into a whole wonderful world of storytelling. If you visit the Ghibli Museum, you'll find a library stocked with scores of recommended children's books, and Hayao Miyazaki himself has published his list of essential reads, making it clear that the films, for all their imagination and ingenuity, didn't simply appear out of nowhere. This is the chapter where we live up to our name. *Ghibliotheque* suggests a Ghibli bibliothèque, and here we're opening the doors of the library to look at the novels adapted by Ghibli, the manga drawn by Miyazaki when he was sharpening his vision, and the books that take us behind the scenes of the studio.

Nausicaä of the Valley of the Wind (manga)

Author: Hayao Miyazaki
First published: 1982–1994

The story of Nausicaä has a fork in its path. There is one road that takes the heroine from her small valley at the edge of a gradually dying world, into the battlegrounds of a war between people and nature, where she emerges as a saviour, filling hearts with harmony, the promise of new life and hope emerging beneath her feet.

That is the road taken by the 1984 film *Nausicaä of the Valley of the Wind*, and it's the one that's most familiar to audiences, but the other road taken, one that's longer, confusing, dark and sublime, is one of Hayao Miyazaki's most entrancing works: the *Nausicaä of the Valley of the Wind* manga.

First published in *Animage* magazine in February 1982, the manga would continue until March 1994, eventually crossing 1,000 pages – the events of the film adaptation being only a small portion of a story that veers into very different territory early in its telling.

After the release, and success, of the *Nausicaä* film and the launch of Studio Ghibli, Miyazaki would work on his manga epic until late at night, perhaps drawn to the freedom and power of controlling every aspect of it, compared to the sprawling, collaborative nature of filmmaking.

Above: Top Spore. Nausicaä's journey brings her into contact with her planet's uncanny flora.

Opposite: While *Nausicaä* manga was drawn in black and white, Miyazaki supplemented the series with vivid, painted artwork for magazine covers and posters.

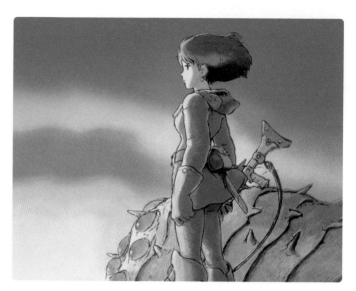

He named his protagonist after a character from Homer's *Odyssey* who delighted in nature, and then drew inspiration for her fascination with all things creepy-crawly from a twelfth-century Japanese story called *The Lady who Loved Insects*. Both characters have pure loves, but are at points powerless, or scorned, by the actions of their societies. In a 1987 article, attached to the first volume of the manga, Miyazaki wrote that in telling this story, with a protagonist inspired by parts of both women, he hoped for "this girl to somehow find freedom and happiness".

But, by the time the saga, which he had called his "most difficult work", was finished, his search hadn't perhaps been as purely fruitful, concluding that he "ended the story at the same as we are now, at the starting point of an incomprehensible world". In the writing of the manga Miyazaki's worldview had changed. He was now more conscious of global conflicts and environmental destruction, and the family-friendly pleasures of *My Neighbour Totoro* (1988) and *Kiki's Delivery Service* (1989) had given way to the threats of *Porco Rosso* (1992) and, soon after, the murky violence

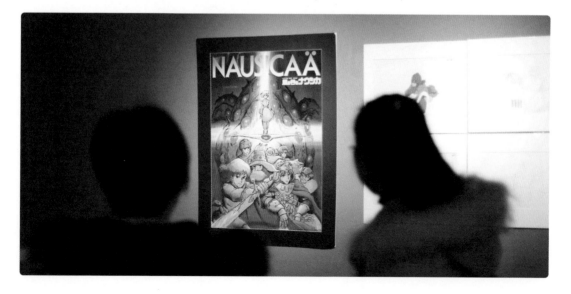

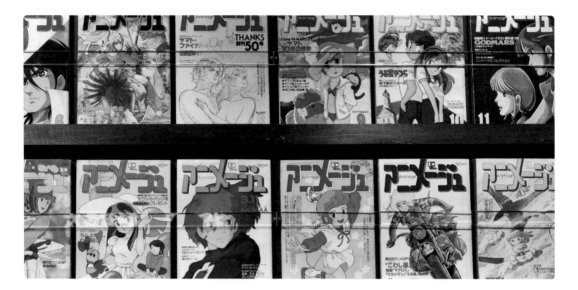

of *Princess Mononoke* (1997). This meant that for Nausicaä, the pure heroine who battles clear evils, she too would have to step into the grey areas of warfare.

The world of the manga is gripping and discombobulating, with Nausicaä's journey being less messianic and more of a coming-of-age story wrapped around a political tinderbox, an expanded map and character list sending her on a quest into different regions, religions and moral quandaries. Rather than profess Nausicaä as a higher power, this story in a way reduces her, and humanity, as less than their world's insect counterparts. In navigating the hierarchy of nature, she humbles herself to her environment, yet also wields a poisonous, radioactive weapon in the form of the infamous God Warrior. Animated by Hideaki Anno (creator of the *Evangelion* series), the God Warrior is a gloopy humanoid bomb in the film, but here becomes a proto-child to Nausicaä and enables her to commit what is, to some readers' interpretation, a genocidal act (the psychoanalysis of the relationship could take up this book). Rather than

arrive at a simple message of hope, Miyazaki forces us to consider all the possible evil in the world and challenges us to survive within it, Nausicaä at one point remarking that "Life is the light that shines in the darkness". (For Miyazaki scholar Susan Napier, that's "the most beautiful line Miyazaki ever wrote".)

It is, in other words, complex, and its ideas linger across Miyazaki's work. Stylistically, the faces offer familiarity, but his drawing is very tight, scratchy and hugely detailed. Compared to the space found in *Shuna's Journey* (1983), the hatched black lines, particularly in busy, discombobulating battle sequences, make the *Nausicaä* manga a much more claustrophobic reading experience. It's in this monochrome madness that Miyazaki teases the intense, limb-ripping violence of *Mononoke*, the creepy, gloopy figures of *Howl's Moving Castle* (2004) and even the liminal, borderless spaces and dream logic of *The Boy and the Heron* (2023).

As the world has become even more incomprehensible than Miyazaki could have imagined, the manifold mysteries of the *Nausicaä* manga have become more valuable. Rather than offering the escape of a clean-cut saviour, we are instead offered the reassurance of someone who has to wrestle with the world, and who doesn't always win. While Nausicaä in the film may have given us a moral compass, here we have a moral map, with infinite routes of traversal.

Above: *Nausicaä* was a popular recurring feature in *Animage* magazine, once edited by Ghibli president, Toshio Suzuki.

Opposite above left: Nausicaä atop her flying machine, on the cover of the manga's first collected tankōbon volume.

Opposite above right: Nausicaä's relationship with the giant creatures becomes intensified in the manga's expanded story.

Opposite below: *Nausicaä* manga remains hugely popular, with artwork appearing in exhibitions.

Shuna's Journey

Author: Hayao Miyazaki
First published: 1983

....

Shuna's Journey is not a long book. You can read the whole story, Hayao Miyazaki's afterword and the 2022 notes from translator Alex Dudok de Wit in less than an hour.

But despite its slender form, the shadow it cast over decades of Ghibli's output is enormous. "*Shuna's Journey* is so much a part of Miyazaki's career ... some of [his films] hark back explicitly to *Shuna's Journey*" Dudok de Wit told us. "It's full of ideas, motifs, images, characters and scenes that are not always fully developed within *Shuna's Journey* but which developed subsequently in his films." So what makes this short story, mostly told with pictures and crumbs of dialogue, so important?

Adapted from a Tibetan folk tale called *The Prince Who Turned into a Dog*, Miyazaki's illustrated book (or "emonogatari") follows a young prince, who leaves his poor and hungry village in the hopes of finding mythical seeds that can help reverse the blight that's attacked his world. Encountering, and helping to free, a young woman soon to be sold into slavery, Shuna journeys beyond the edge of his world to a cursed Eden and back again.

Created after *Lupin III: The Castle of Cagliostro* (1979), *Shuna's Journey* was published between the release of the first edition of the *Nausicaä* manga and its subsequent 1984 film adaptation, and it's clear to see the creative cross-pollination between them and other Ghibli works. On the page *Shuna* is very different to *Nausicaä*. Compared to the latter's dark convolutions in both style and story, *Shuna's* bright, colourful watercolour approach savours large open spaces, the sparing words offering only the minimum necessary exposition. Some ideas, however, seep between stories. An opening image of a small village nestled in a valley (one where a youthful hero combating perishing resources is resident) is replicated in *Nausicaä*; the image of a mysterious ship resting in the dunes of a large desert would return in *Tales From Earthsea* (the 2006 film credits *Shuna* as well as Ursula K. Le Guin's novels for inspiration); the ethereal sight of ancient, enormous amphibians would resurface in *Ponyo* (2008); and the elk-like Yakul would become a companion again in 1997 in *Princess Mononoke* (here a species, there an individual name).

This is not to say the book is an unpolished sketchbook for Miyazaki; it is a great work in itself, outside of its various contextual curiosities. The light touches of text emphasizes the imagery, the refreshing watercolours bringing to life rich tableaux and striking portraits, held by faces with rounder, warmer features befitting the tale's fable-like, abstractly child-friendly nature. Although brisk, it still manages to explore weighty topics like slavery, greed and trauma, its image-focused, emotion-focused form offering swifter clarity than any words might. If you haven't already, take an hour to read *Shuna's Journey*; it's a small but powerful seedbed for Ghibli and many mighty stories have sprung from its roots.

Opposite: A classic (re)discovered. The cover of Alex Dudok de Wit's landmark English-language translation of *Shuna's Journey*.

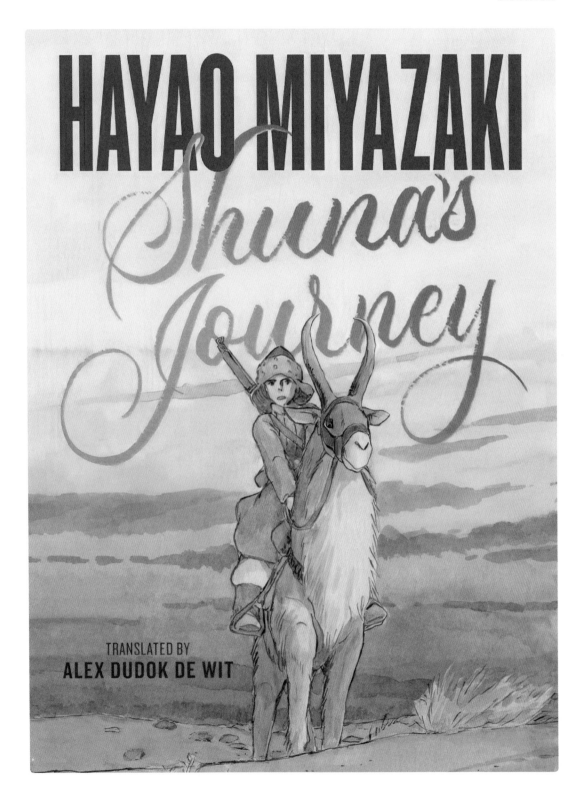

HAYAO MIYAZAKI
Shuna's Journey

TRANSLATED BY
ALEX DUDOK DE WIT

Kiki's Delivery Service

Author: Eiko Kadono
First published: 1985

....

**While *Kiki's Delivery Service* will always be closely associated
with Studio Ghibli's 1989 hit animation, Eiko Kadono's novel has
had a long and illustrious life of its own.**

The book has inspired everything from live-action
film adaptations to stage musicals to even a whole
museum, Kiki's Museum of Literature, which opened
in Edogawa City in 2023, and houses a collection of
10,000 children's books.

And yet author Eiko Kadono is often overshadowed
by Hayao Miyazaki when it comes to discussion of Kiki
and her enduring appeal. Following the first Kiki book
in 1985, Kadono continued the story of the little witch
across several sequels, watching the character grow
through her teenage years and into adulthood and
even parenthood. In 2018, she was awarded the Hans
Christian Andersen Award, joining other legendary
honorees such as Astrid Lindgren, Tove Jansson and
Maurice Sendak. The awarding body, the International
Board on Books for Young People, described
Kadono's work as "always surprising, engaging, and
empowering. And almost always fun. And always
life affirming."

Thankfully, a new English-language translation of
Kiki's Delivery Service was published in 2020 and
gave readers the chance to discover both the story
as originally conceived and the inimitable touch of
its original author. This breezy, episodic, slice-of-life
version of *Kiki's Delivery Service* doesn't have the
emotional conflict or the high-flying final act peril of
Miyazaki's film. Instead, it gently progresses through
the seasons, following Kiki as she beds into her new
hometown of Koriko, sets up her shop, crafts her own
broom, and helps out the locals as best she can, with
the jeopardy levels rarely surpassing the danger of
the town clocktower's bell missing its annual chimes
at midnight on New Year's Eve. Jiji the cat, Osono the
baker and the awkward boy Tombo (who, spoiler

alert, eventually becomes Kiki's husband) are all here.
Kiki even visits home at the end, after one whole year
of independence, to check in on her parents, before
returning to Koriko and realizing that she has made her
own home for herself there.

Born in 1935, Kadono was something of a late
bloomer: her first book was published when she was

Above: Queen Witch. Eiko Kadono, legendary author of *Kiki's
Delivery Service* and almost 200 other books.

Opposite: The cover of Kiki's first adventure, which has since
inspired a live-action film and a stage play as well as Miyazaki's
1989 animation.

35, but she mostly wrote in private and became a professional author only seven years later. The inspiration for *Kiki's Delivery Service* came from her 12-year-old daughter, who one day filled a piece of paper with doodles of witches. One in particular intrigued Kadono: the image of a witch and black cat on a broom, with a radio dangling underneath. In 2020, she told Tor.com, "I thought, it would probably feel great to fly along listening to something like 'The Long and Winding Road' by The Beatles."

While her storytelling instincts may differ from Hayao Miyazaki's, the two share a similar knack for finding ways to ground fantastical concepts in ways that are tangible, recognizable, relatable. In her introduction to the 2020 English-language edition of her novel, Kadono lays out her thinking behind giving her witch one simple talent: that of flight. "Kiki's magic is as close to normal as possible – it's everyday magic," she explains. "She is a witch but she's also a perfectly ordinary girl. She has the same worries, disappointments and joys as anyone else... I've come to believe that everyone has some type of magic inside them. If a person can find their magic and lovingly cultivate it, they'll truly feel alive every day. There is magic inside each and every one of you, too – I believe that."

Above: Well Read. Opened in 2023, Kiki's Museum of Literature in Tokyo is crammed with 10,000 books.

Right: International translations of *Kiki's Delivery Service*, including the recent American and British editions.

Howl's Moving Castle

Author: Diana Wynne Jones
First published: 1986

The film of *Howl's Moving Castle* was a troubled production, not least because Hayao Miyazaki came out of retirement to wrest the director's chair away from Ghibli newcomer Mamoru Hosoda (more on that in Chapter Seven: Next Ghibli).

Pick up Diana Wynne Jones's book, however, and all the angst and anguish of the adaptation (both off- and on-screen) melt away.

Her *Howl's Moving Castle* is warm, eccentric, dry-humoured and full of delightful details. It's powered by the simple yet alluring premise that its story takes place in a land of magic, Ingary, "where such things as seven-league boots and cloaks of invisibility really exist". Yet Sophie Hatter, the eldest child of a well-to-do family, thinks she has no hope of an interesting future – until she meets the Witch of the Waste and, later, the Wizard Howl. While it's a work of singular imagination,

it's also in dialogue with the tropes of fantasy literature, which are gently subverted or made new, in a similar way to another wise and witty riff on the fantasy tradition, the novel *Stardust* by Neil Gaiman who is a professed admirer of Wynne's work.

Below (left): The first American edition of *Howl's Moving Castle*. The frightful look is courtesy of illustrator Jos. A. Smith.

Below (right): Diana Wynne Jones continued the stories of Howl and Sophie in the books *Castle in the Air* and *House of Many Ways*.

Opposite: Contrary to Wynne Jones's intentions, the wizard Howl has become an object of affection the world over.

The world of Miyazaki's *Howl's Moving Castle* is ravaged by war, which is something that merely brews in the background of the book. The director brought it front and centre as he worked through his feelings about American imperialism and the War on Terror. Howl is embroiled in conflict and has been cursed for it – something that drags the adaptation down into doldrums much deeper than the source novel. Wynne Jones herself described having a "faint miffed feeling" when watching the film, remarking that Miyazaki had introduced his "favourite obsessions", and perceptively identified that while she and Miyazaki are members of the same post-war generation, they approach the spectre of the Second World War differently. "I tend to leave the actual war out (we all know how horrible wars are)," she remarks in an afterword, "whereas Miyazaki (who feels just the same) has his cake and eats it, representing both the nastiness of a war and the exciting scenic effects of a big bombing raid."

Wynne Jones has said that the initial inspiration for the Wizard Howl came from her stroppy teenage son, something that becomes all too clear when Howl's decidedly unmagical roots are revealed. Miyazaki neglects to include this twist, that the Wizard is in fact an ordinary Welsh man named Howell Jenkins, turned fantasy antihero after giving his heart to the fire demon Calcifer. (We can't resist noting, too, that Miyazaki

elected to change the name of Howl's apprentice, Michael, to the more exotic Markl. We'll try not to take it personally.) When it came to designing the animated version of Howl, producer Toshio Suzuki said that Wynne Jones's model for the character was musical icon David Bowie – but Miyazaki, remarkably, had never heard of the rock star. Nevertheless, however ambivalent the intended characterization, Howl on screen became the peak of problematic faves, a gloomy goth boyfriend beloved by impressionable viewers around the world.

Of all the effects of having your work brought to the big screen by Studio Ghibli, Wynne Jones told *Publisher's Weekly* that the most pronounced was the exponential rise of adoring Howl superfans. "The procession of people, which was enormous already, has increased — doubled and tripled — of all the people who want to marry Howl," she said. "Now it seems to me that Howl would be one of the most dreadful husbands one could possibly imagine. But there are these thousands of girls who write and say 'Is Howl real? I want to marry him.' All around the world."

Above: They're floating in a most peculiar way. Sophie and Howl, whose look was inspired by David Bowie, leap through the sky.

Earwig and the Witch
Author: Diana Wynne Jones
First published: 2011

Much like its Ghibli counterpart, *Earwig and the Witch* is something of an odd entry in an otherwise revered body of work. Released in June 2011, mere months after the death of author Diana Wynne Jones, the novel is short, lopsided, perhaps even unfinished. The tale of an unruly girl adopted by two fearsome foster parents, and the battle for supremacy waged between them within the walls of their strange magical bungalow may be a little undercooked, but it is nevertheless a bite-sized delight.

Written in Wynne Jones's unfussy style, the book is laced with dry humour drawn from its eccentric characters and the incongruous mix of the magical and the mundane, from the Bella Yaga's thoroughly unremarkable book of spells ("to win first prize in a dog show"; "to make a skateboard do tricks"; "to make next door's dahlias die") to the Mandrake's taste for bland, everyday dishes served up by diabolical means ("pie and chips from Stoke-on-Trent station... it's my favourite food").

You can easily see what attracted Studio Ghibli to the material, not least the chance to add a decidedly disobedient female protagonist to the company's roster of characters. Yet Gorō Miyazaki's adaptation struggled on many fronts: adding rock-band flourishes, attempting to fill in the narrative gaps left by the author, and breaking new stylistic ground with a 3DCG animated approach that never quite balanced the photorealistic and the grotesque. In contrast, Diana Wynne Jones's novel, as compromised as it is, has an easy, confident and compelling charm.

Below (left): Published posthumously, *Earwig and the Witch* was a slight, but charming, addition to Diana Wynne Jones's bibliography.

Below (right): While *Howl's Moving Castle* was a hit, Gorō's take on *Earwig and the Witch* fared less well.

The Borrowers

Author: Mary Norton
First published: 1952

....

In the production notes for _Arrietty_, producer Toshio Suzuki reveals that both Hayao Miyazaki and Isao Takahata had previously considered adapting Mary Norton's _Borrowers_ stories decades before the task fell to first-time director Hiromasa Yonebayashi.

On reading the books themselves, that comes as no surprise, given how fascinated both are with the everyday lives of their characters. These books embrace the details and habits of the Borrowers, only inches tall and living under the floorboards of a household, surviving on scraps scavenged from the residents above.

Mary Norton's inspiration for her series of novels chimes perfectly with Miyazaki's own irresistible cocktail of observation and imagination. As she relates in an introduction to the collected _Borrowers_ stories, Norton was a child prone to daydreaming – or, as she herself describes, "an inveterate lingerer, a gazer into banks and hedgerows, a rapt investigator of shallow pools, a lier-down by teeming ditches." One day, she found herself wondering, "what would it be like... to live among such creatures – human oneself to all intents and purposes, but as small and vulnerable as they? What would one live on? Where make one's home? Which would be enemies and which would be friends?"

Miyazaki's own process-driven creative mind is just as interested in the mechanics of a Moving Castle, or the workings of a young boy's toy boat made life-size – and you can see this reflected in Norton's vision for her own fictional world. Ultimately, she asserts, they are "very practical" books, born out of dreaming up "commando-like assault courses" for her characters, imagining how they would venture "from window-seat to bedside table without touching the floor".

What's delightful about _The Borrowers_ on the page is the attention to these tiny details, with paragraphs given over to how these characters fashion a working kitchen out of scavenged materials, or prepare for the epic expedition of traversing the human household. The adventure grows out of everyday settings, which brings

to mind a moment in the documentary _The Kingdom of Dreams and Madness_ in which Miyazaki gazes out of the window at a mundane urban landscape, imagining an acrobatic hero leaping between the rooftops.

In the process of adaptation, director Hiromasa Yonebayashi retained that sense of adventure, but added extra peril in the telling, which is most apparent in Arrietty's hair-raising scrapes with the household's gigantic pet cat, and the disaster-movie spectacle of meddlesome housekeeper Haru's discovery of the Borrowers' family home. The film also depicts Shō, the young human who befriends Arrietty, as a crucial couple of years older – more of a contemporary, perhaps even a young love interest – compared to the book's unpredictable, immature and unnamed ten-year-old boy.

These embellishments, not to mention the resetting of the action in Tokyo, close to Ghibli's own office, make _Arrietty_ its own unique beast. However, as with other books translated by Miyazaki into animation, you can find traces of Norton's curious, eccentric, wholly captivating work throughout his films, from a Make Do and Mend anti-consumerist spirit to a worldview marked by the events of the Second World War. But it's Miyazaki's keen interest in magical worlds just out of sight, hidden in the cracks between our everyday lives, that seems to be closest to Norton's vision for the Borrowers. As she describes it, "In the dull, safe routine of those nursery years, it was exciting to imagine there were others in the house, unguessed at by the adult human beings, who were living so close but so dangerously."

Opposite: The Puffin Classics edition of _The Borrowers_, with illustrator Diana Stanley's cover capturing the small-scale world of Arrietty and family.

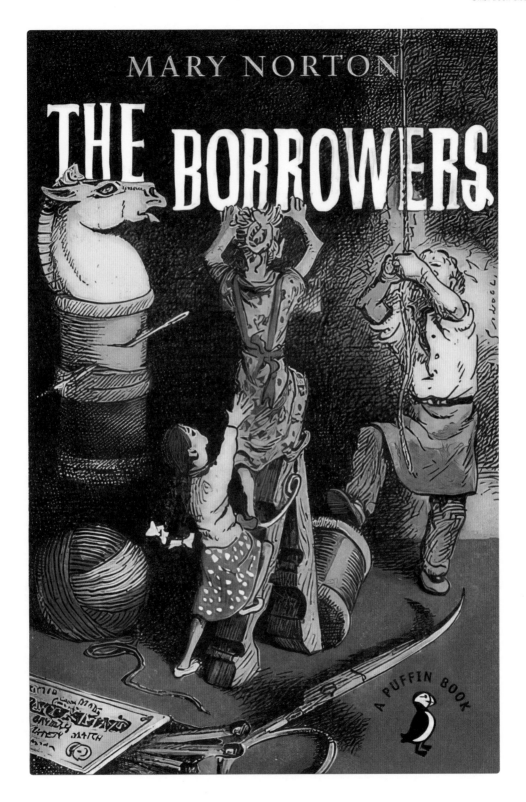

A Wizard of Earthsea

Author: Ursula K. Le Guin
First published: 1968

It's unfortunate that discussion of the relationship between Studio Ghibli and the *Earthsea* novels by Ursula K. Le Guin often gets stuck on the controversial, ill-fated and underrated (if you ask Jake) 2006 feature *Tales From Earthsea*, because the connections run deep.

Part of the stated reason that Hayao Miyazaki eventually decided not to adapt *Earthsea*, and therefore leave the director's chair open for his son, Gorō, was that he had felt that he'd already done so, in a more roundabout way, by drawing inspiration from Le Guin's novels for the likes of *Nausicaä of the Valley of the Wind* (1984), *Princess Mononoke* (1997) and *Spirited Away* (2001). And besides, he'd retired from filmmaking – temporarily.

Whether you enjoyed *Tales From Earthsea* or not – or even if you haven't seen it at all – it is worth seeking out Le Guin's *Earthsea*, which came to encompass an

expansive canon of five novels and seven short stories released over the course of 50 years. *A Wizard of Earthsea*, the first book-length story, is as radical and wise as it was on the day of its first publication in 1968. It's a coming-of-age story following Ged, a gifted

Below (left): The first edition of *A Wizard of Earthsea*, featuring artwork from Ruth Robbins.

Below (right): Author Ursula K. Le Guin's influence across science fiction and fantasy storytelling is impossible to quantify.

Opposite: Gorō Miyazaki's controversial adaptation *Tales from Earthsea* may be majestic, but some believe it misunderstands the novel's themes.

young wizard who wrestles with pride, shame and the consequences of his actions after he brings a shadow creature into the world. His journey of self-discovery and, ultimately, self-acceptance takes him to the far reaches of Earthsea, as he hones his talents and expands his horizons, coming into contact with various disparate communities of people along the way.

A Wizard of Earthsea is a work of great imagination, wisdom and vision. Le Guin's dense prose reads like an ancient epic, filled with history, language, lore and landscape, but the book's progressive ideas are expressed with clarity. This may be a fantasy story populated with wizards and dragons, but Le Guin rejects the simple paradigm of good versus evil for a

more complex, personal framework: a relationship with darkness, rather than a fight against it. There are no easy villains; instead Ged must reckon with internal conflicts, and understand his connection with the wider world. It's a journey not too dissimilar from that of Ashitaka and San in Princess Mononoke: two young protagonists poised between warring factions, heirs to a doomed world, tasked with finding peace and balance within it.

Even in a world filled with magic, there is nothing more powerful in Earthsea than knowing a person's, or being's, true name. "Who knows a man's true name," Le Guin writes, "holds that man's life in his keeping." Miyazaki borrowed this notion for Spirited Away –

it's what gives Yubaba such power over Haku – but Le Guin goes further. The grand finale of the book, Ged's meeting with his shadow self, is no spectacular showdown, but instead a quiet, resolute moment of communion. In giving his shadow his own name, Ged "had neither lost nor won, but... had made himself whole: a man: who, knowing his whole true self, cannot be used or possessed by any power other than himself."

Reading the source novel brings into sharp relief the failings of Ghibli's own take on *Earthsea*, of which Le Guin was always the sharpest and most discerning critic. When delivering her assessment of the film on her own website in 2006, she wrote: "Much of it was exciting. The excitement was maintained by violence,

to a degree that I find deeply untrue to the spirit of the books." She also took exception to the creation of an outright villain for the film, the evil wizard Cob. "The darkness within us can't be done away with by swinging a magic sword... In modern fantasy (literary or governmental), killing people is the usual solution to the so-called war between good and evil. My books are not conceived in terms of such a war, and offer no simple answers to simplistic questions."

Opposite: Ghibli's exploration of Earthsea isn't particularly beloved, but its landscapes and settings are a consistent highlight.

Right: Regularly bathed in golden light, what the film lacks in storytelling nuance it (almost) makes up for in beauty.

When Marnie Was There

Author: Joan G. Robinson
First published: 1967

When it was first announced that Studio Ghibli were making *When Marnie Was There* into a film, the source novel was surprisingly tricky to track down in English.

Despite acclaim following its publication in 1967 and subsequent adaptations for television and radio, Joan G. Robinson's *Marnie* was out of circulation. When it was published in a new edition in 2014, just shy of the Japanese release of the Ghibli film, the author's daughter Deborah Sheppard wrote in the afterword about the novel's enduring appeal to readers from Japan. She recalled an occasion when a Japanese tourist was able to navigate his way from London all the way to Burnham Overy, the real-life Norfolk town that inspired the fictional setting of Little Overton. As she notes, "all he had was a copy of the book as his guide." And so, in a way, Ghibli's adaptation repaid the favour, and brought a new generation of readers to Robinson's work.

Marnie (as it was called, until the release of the Alfred Hitchcock film of the same name prompted a last-minute title change) was close to Robinson's heart. It was reportedly the favourite of all her books, and was inspired by the coastal landscape that she called home. Hiromasa Yonebayashi's film sensitively captures the loneliness and yearning of the story's young protagonist, Anna, and her uncanny friendship with a mysterious girl who has slipped through the cracks of time, but Robinson's original has textures impossible to translate.

The author's prose is peppered with local vernacular and detailed descriptions of seaside nature that give the novel a distinctive sense of place. The pages

Below (left): Illustrator Peggy Fortnum's evocative work can also be seen in certain editions of Michael Bond's Paddington Bear stories.

Below (right): Hiromasa Yonebayashi's adaptation moved the action to Japan, but lost none of the novel's melancholy feel.

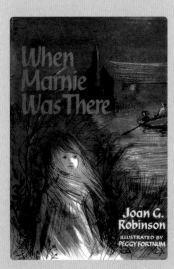

ring with the sound of sandpipers ("Pity me! Oh, pity me!"), the "soughing of the wind in the marram grasses" and the "mad, scary, scatterbrained cry" of peewits. Robinson also introduces the inescapable (and inescapably British) theme of class, and teases out these subtle cultural markers of difference, from bingo nights and boxing on the TV to an evening meal, "tea", that is described as "a mountain of baked beans, a kipper and a sticky iced bun". In contrast to the more down-to-earth local way of life, the Lindsays, who move into Marnie's abandoned house, are immediately identified as "London people, but not the kind who made themselves unpopular in the village".

There is much to uncover, too, in the book's rawer, more tortured portrayal of its protagonist. While the film lifts a handy visual metaphor of the invisible social

circles and boundaries that can make someone feel "inside" or "outside", Anna's loneliness is thornier, more unpredictable. She is often so overcome with anxiety and angst that she can't help but lash out at other residents of the town, even those with good intentions. Ultimately, she does find herself "inside", but only after her experiences with Marnie, and after finding out the truth behind their extraordinary connection. Accompanied by pen-scratch illustrations by Peggy Fortnum which accentuate the hazy, dreamlike, almost sepulchral tones of the story, Robinson's book is wise and wonderful in its own distinctive way – a treasure worth discovering.

Above: A wall display of sketches from an exhibition of artwork from the Ghibli adaptation of *When Marnie Was There*.

How Do You Live?

Author: Genzaburo Yoshino
First Published: 1937

Of course, we now know that Hayao Miyazaki's long-gestating feature *The Boy and the Heron* is not, in fact, an animated adaptation of the Japanese novel *How Do You Live?* Instead, Miyazaki merely borrowed the title — Kimitachi wa Dō Ikiru ka — for the film's Japanese release.

But it's hard to forget that, for years, it was presumed that Genzaburo Yoshino's novel was the source for the filmmaker's so-called swansong. Such is the power of Miyazaki and Studio Ghibli that even the *suggestion* that the director was adapting a relatively obscure Japanese book from the 1930s could result in multiple reprintings, unprecedented international translations, and close to two million copies sold in Japan alone.

However, close to the 2023 release of *The Boy and the Heron*, producer Toshio Suzuki made it clear that the novel played only a part in the film, though its appearance is far from insignificant. As the young protagonist, Mahito, is mourning the loss of his mother, he sorts through a pile of books left by her specifically for him, with *How Do You Live?* being the most visible. That striking title acts as a focal point for a central theme not only of this particular film but of Miyazaki's late career as a whole: how to find a meaningful and moral way of living in uncertain times.

And yet, despite what Suzuki says, the connections and crossover between the book and the filmmaker go further than just the title. *How Do You Live?* is as much a coming-of-age story as it is an entire educational syllabus that encompasses art, science, language, history, ethics and philosophy, explored through the everyday experiences of one schoolboy, Copper, and his correspondence with his uncle, who has an essay or thought-provoking anecdote for any and every occasion.

Like many of Miyazaki's works, the book is focused on young minds as they're still taking shape, and as they develop self-awareness, independence and emotional intelligence. As Copper learns life lessons and stands up to feelings of fear and shame, you can see so much of Kiki, Chihiro, Ashitaka and San. At the heart of it all is a sense of intergenerational exchange between uncle and nephew, author and reader. It brings to mind Miyazaki's proposal for *Whisper of the Heart*, in which he wrote that "this film will represent a type of challenge issued by a bunch of middle-aged men... to today's young people. It will attempt to stimulate a spiritual thirst, and convey the importance of yearning and aspiration to an audience that... tends to give up too easily on the idea of being the stars of their own stories".

The title of the book is a question, but it is also a challenge to the reader to take what they will from the work at hand, and apply it to their own life, whether that's a teachable moment from Copper's schooldays, or a wayward digression on the life of Napoleon. To quote Neil Gaiman, who was tasked with writing an introduction to the novel in anticipation of an adaptation that never came: "this is such a strange book, and such a wise book".

Opposite: The Japanese cover for *How Do You Live?* from the *Nihon shōkokumin bunko* series (Library of Books for Young People of Japan).

Michael's Ghibli Bookshelf

As you can tell by now, we love books, and we love books both by and about Studio Ghibli. When we first started the Ghibliotheque project, there weren't many Ghibli-related books available in English, but thankfully that situation is changing with each passing year. If you're looking to build a library like ours, here are a dozen or so recommendations to get you started...

Starting Point 1979–1996 / Turning Point 1997–2008
Author: Hayao Miyazaki

Two volumes of collected essays, interviews, press conferences, project proposals and "directorial memoranda" covering Hayao Miyazaki's career, from formative influences and early works, through the foundation and rise of Studio Ghibli, to the production of *Ponyo* in 2008. Essential reading for anyone wishing to go deeper into the mind, worldview and creative process of the legendary director.

The Ghibli Art Series

These lush coffee-table books compile all forms of artwork that go into creating a Ghibli feature film, from storyboards, to design sketches, to painted backgrounds, to the finished film stills. Each volume offers a consummate showcase of the many talented hands behind the work – just pick your favourite film, and dive in. And if you want to go deeper, try importing the full e-conte storyboard books from Japan.

Princess Mononoke: The First Story
Author: Hayao Miyazaki

When Hayao Miyazaki started development on the feature project that would become *Princess Mononoke* (1997), Ghibli published this collection of artwork from his first, aborted attempt to make a film under that name over a decade previously. Essentially Miyazaki's spin on *Beauty and the Beast*, this picture book is an intriguing and entertaining look at what could have been – and, in its grinning, catlike design of the rotund Mononoke, points the way to Totoro.

Nausicaä of the Valley of the Wind: Watercolour Impressions
Author: Hayao Miyazaki

This gorgeous volume collects artwork created by Hayao Miyazaki from across the whole span of his years creating *Nausicaä*, from colour pages created for the manga to image board paintings and design sketches for the film. Most fascinating, though, is a section charting "the way to Nausicaä", which brings together disparate sketches and ideas from the early 1980s, allowing us to witness Miyazaki mashing together influences from Japanese history, sci-fi, fantasy and fairy tale as he found his own signature style.

Mixing Work With Pleasure: My Life at Studio Ghibli
Author: Toshio Suzuki

It often falls to producer Toshio Suzuki to be Ghibli's spokesperson and yarn-spinner, and he's happily fulfilled that function for decades. This slim but valuable volume offers his perspective on everything from his role in getting *Nausicaä of the Valley of the Wind* off the ground, to his insights into the working practices of both Miyazaki and Takahata, to his management of the often tricky process of handing the baton over to a younger generation of filmmakers.

Grave of the Fireflies
Author: Alex Dudok de Wit

In the English-speaking world, Hayao Miyazaki's work tends to loom large, so there are very few books that examine the films of his colleague and former mentor, Isao Takahata. This insightful entry in the BFI Film Classics series from animation critic Alex Dudok de Wit is the rare exception and offers a rounded and exhaustively researched analysis of a film often dismissed (however positively) as an anti-war weepie.

Sharing a House with the Never-Ending Man: 15 Years at Studio Ghibli
Author: Steve Alpert

Sparky and full to the brim with anecdotes, this insider memoir comes from Ghibli's former "resident foreigner", Steve Alpert, who was tasked with helping the studio break America. The juiciest sections are those related to the release of *Princess Mononoke* and Ghibli's dealings with Disney and Harvey Weinstein's Miramax, but Alpert also provides a sensitive snapshot of Japanese business practices and corporate structure to reveal the realities behind a working studio.

Miyazakiworld: A Life in Art
Author: Susan Napier

Part-biography, part-critical study, this book by academic Susan Napier is an accessible and engaging overview of Miyazaki's whole career, from birth to his beginnings at Toei Animation, and then his success as an animator and filmmaker. It benefits from a broader view, too, taking into account his published writing and manga work, including the epic *Nausicaä of the Valley of the Wind* series.

The Anime Encyclopedia
Authors: Jonathan Clements and Helen McCarthy

If you fancy venturing outside of Studio Ghibli and into deeper waters of Japanese animation, here's the place to start. Clements and McCarthy, two of the UK's leading anime historians, joined forces to compile this exhaustive encyclopedia – now on its 3rd revised edition, with an even further expanded digital version. Then, continue with the authors' solo works, such as Clements' *Anime: A History* and McCarthy's *The Art of Osamu Tezuka: God of Manga* and *Hayao Miyazaki: Master of Japanese Animation*.

Spirited Away
Author: Andrew Osmond

It may be one of Ghibli's most celebrated and globally renowned works, but the production of *Spirited Away* was far from simple, as is covered in this BFI Film Classics volume by critic Andrew Osmond – including the crisis point where Miyazaki was faced with the dawning realization that his fertile imagination was on course to create a film three hours long, prompting a drastic rethink (centring on a background character, No-Face).

My Neighbour Totoro Soundtrack
Author: Kunio Hara

The part played by Joe Hisaishi's music in the enduring appeal of Studio Ghibli's films cannot be understated. This entry in the $33^{1/3}$ series of monographs analyzing great albums and recorded works provides a close reading of his groundbreaking and endlessly catchy score, and stands out from the crowd in being written from the perspective of music history and theory, thanks to expert analysis from academic Kunio Hara.

Studio Ghibli: An Industrial History
Author: Rayna Denison

Rayna Denison is one of the leading voices in anime academia, and this book is a rare study of Ghibli as a functioning business, looking at the important role played by merchandise, advertising and other seldom talked-about projects that paid the bills. See also: the academic essay collection *Princess Mononoke: Understanding Studio Ghibli's Monster Princess*, edited by Denison.

6

Ghibli Documentaries

Behind the scenes of the world's greatest animation studio.

If you're curious to learn just how the artists at Studio Ghibli make their magical films, well, you're in luck. There are few filmmakers or studios who have been as well documented on film or on video. Several in-depth feature-length documentaries – some even longer! – have been made about Hayao Miyazaki, Isao Takahata, their work, their inspirations and their collaborators. In fact, visit the shops at the Ghibli Museum and Ghibli Park and you will find a whole section dedicated to Ghibli docs, many of which remain unreleased and untranslated for international audiences, including titles released in the special *Ghibli ga Ippai* collection, which fittingly translates as "lots of Ghibli". These are the documentaries that launched a thousand "grumpy Miyazaki" memes, and took us behind the curtain to see these wizards at work.

Journey of the Heart

EPISODES:

**Saint-Exupéry: A Dream for the Sky –
From Southern France to Sahara (44 mins, 1998)**

**Dialogue with a Man Who Planted a Canadian Tree
(44 mins, 1999)**

....

Airing between 1993 and 2003, *Journey of the Heart* was a
travel documentary TV series that broadcast on the channel NHK
BS2 in Japan. The format saw celebrities traversing the globe,
following the footsteps of figures who influenced their lives, and
two episodes will catch the attention of any Ghibli fan.

Captured in documentary, whether that is in *The
Kingdom of Dreams and Madness* (2013), *Never-
Ending Man* (2016) or other Ghibli-focused
works, Hayao Miyazaki and Isao Takahata are
predominantly working. Researching, drawing or
casting, they are figures bound to their production
company, so the joy of *Journey of the Heart* is seeing
them separated from their office jobs. Two episodes
of the series saw Miyazaki and Takahata take on
their own individual voyages, away from Ghibli –
and in seeing the directors parted from the studio, a
sharpened portrait of them as artists emerges.

Naturally, Miyazaki's is all about planes. In *Saint-
Exupéry: A Dream for the Sky*, he follows his hero, the
pilot and writer Antoine de Saint-Exupéry. Best known
for beloved classic *The Little Prince*, Saint-Exupéry
delivered air mail from France to the Sahara in the
1920s, and Miyazaki retraces his flight path, illustrated
in *Indiana Jones*-style red lines on a map. Travelling in
planes dating from the early twentieth century and now
restored, including one that's the same red as Porco
Rosso's seaplane, a youthfully grey and distinctly gruff
Miyazaki dissolves into an excitable schoolboy with
every glance at a propeller, or peek through an aerial
window. We have known his love for flight through
his work, but it feels special to see him in the presence
of his passion, enveloped by his subject rather than
capturing it. Miyazaki's pilgrimage ends at the desert

airfield of Cap Juby, where Saint-Exupéry was based,
and it's here that it becomes clear just how much his
hero's life means to him. The familiar full smile, sharp
with regular words of apocalyptic dread, is no more,
Miyazaki becoming overwhelmed by the golden
dusted setting. "It's more beautiful than I could have
imagined," he says, and to see him experience this
connection is almost the same.

Takahata's episode, *Dialogue with a Man Who
Planted a Canadian Tree*, keeps things closer to the
ground. The director travels to Canada to meet with
animator Frédéric Back, Academy Award winner for
his short film *Crac* (1981), a story about a rocking
chair experiencing industrialization, which was solely
animated by Back himself. Prior to meeting Back,
Takahata begins his journey in the Prince Edward
Island forest, the setting of his TV series *Anne of Green
Gables* (1979). Revisiting and discussing locations
from the work, the gentle, wise figure of Takahata
is so natural walking and talking to camera that he
could've considered a late-stage career change as a
TV presenter. It's a delight to see how he went about
adapting interesting, albeit slightly underwhelming,
aspects of Prince Edward Island, rescaling and
reimagining them to fit the wide-eyed wonder of
his show. Elsewhere, a visit to a historical village
shows Takahaya delighting in traditional agricultural
methods, while a visit to a native community shows

his passion for maintaining local culture, whether in sculpture, language or dance. It's in his conversations with Back that we glean the most of Takahata the filmmaker. Back is the lone creator of his films, whereas Takahata doesn't animate on any of his, yet the two artists are so aligned in their practice and philosophy. Whether sketching them or conducting them, these

are artists focused on drawing and redrawing direct lines between the power of nature and its delicately balanced relationship to humanity.

Above: The DVD cover of the two *Journey of the Heart* documentaries, in which Miyazaki and Takahata connected with their inspirations.

The Kingdom of Dreams and Madness

Directed by: Mami Sunada
Length: 118 mins / Year: 2013

If you watch one documentary about Studio Ghibli, make it this one. Mami Sunada's wonderful film stands apart from the crowd thanks to her light touch, observational style and fly-on-the-wall approach to capturing the studio at work.

It's also, in stark contrast to some of the specials and series included in this chapter, a *feature film* documentary in both runtime and execution.

Just shy of two hours long, it has the sharp, specific focus of following the studio as both Hayao Miyazaki and Isao Takahata worked on what, at that time, were believed to be their "final" films, *The Wind Rises* (2013) and *The Tale of the Princess Kaguya* (2013). Sunada was initially commissioned by Disney Japan to create

a promotional behind-the-scenes documentary for the pair of films, but she had other ideas. She was fresh off the release of her acclaimed debut film, *Ending Note: Death of a Japanese Salaryman* (2011), a moving

Opposite: Power trio. This half-photograph, half-painting shows the three key figures of the Ghibliverse: Hayao Miyazaki, Toshio Suzuki and Isao Takahata.

Below: Blue-sky thinking. Miyazaki ends the day with a cigarette break on the Ghibli office roof terrace.

portrait of the final months of her father's life, and she presented Toshio Suzuki with an unprecedented pitch: rather than a TV programme or DVD bonus feature, why not make a documentary for release in cinemas? This impressed the producer. "There's been a lot of coverage in the history of Studio Ghibli," Sunada recalled him telling her. "But you're the first to say you want to make a MOVIE."

For close to a year, Sunada visited Studio Ghibli HQ almost every day. She had her own desk, she ate lunch with Ghibli colleagues and was even ferried home by Toshio Suzuki. Such unprecedented access is hard to come by, and Sunada's film has an easy atmosphere that can only come from a warm welcome. The film's opening frames feature gentle pans across establishing shots of the Ghibli Museum and the main studio office, as Masakatsu Takagi's melodic score ebbs and flows in the background. Much like Sunada herself, we're beckoned inside, as the director shares with us her personal journal of her time at the studio.

It takes great skill to achieve such a breezy tone, and there's great craft and vision behind Sunada's film. Despite the historic double bill on the release slate, the director is not overwhelmed by the importance and legacy of the studio and its founding filmmakers. Sunada provides context and the briefest of narration only where necessary, and instead finds stray moments in the everyday bustle of the studio which speak volumes about the creative process and the idiosyncrasies of Studio Ghibli as a workplace and a community – such as a team taking time out of the day to head up to the roof terrace to observe a particularly beautiful sunset.

In fact, it might be better to say that Sunada approaches Ghibli as one giant family. *The Kingdom of Dreams and Madness* has a similar intimacy and sensitivity to her debut, and her apprenticeship with Japanese director Hirokazu Kore-eda (*Still Walking*, *Shoplifters*), master of the delicate domestic drama, is also reflected in this studio snapshot. While the assembled staff are working away on yet another animated masterpiece, they fill their days with routines and rituals, from coordinated callisthenics programmes to regular deliveries of Yakult.

This "family" has three parents: Hayao Miyazaki, decked out in his work apron; Toshio Suzuki, the problem-solving producer who, say staff, "would make a good detective"; and finally, the elusive Isao Takahata, who is working at his own pace on the other side of town. Sunada's unobtrusive shooting style – literally just her and a small handheld camera – brings her (and us) closer than ever before to the people behind the studio. Where other Ghibli documentaries are built on interviews, this one feels moulded together from hushed conversations and small talk between colleagues, over the desk, over the course of their work days.

Sunada also has a masterful eye for a cutaway, inserting delightful little shots that, like the best Ghibli films, focus on the details. Handwritten notes and doodles on desks, dappled sunlight on the wall, a Totoro plushie positioned at the head of a meeting room table – all these add colour and shading to an already fully rounded picture. And, of course, there's breakout star Ushiko, Studio Ghibli's resident cat, who skulks about the place, coming and going as she pleases, with, as Miyazaki himself remarks, "no schedule". Something you could say about the director of this delightful documentary.

Of course, there are many "making of" titbits here for fans to chew on. In one sequence, we have a front row seat to the discussions around who could provide the perfect voice for the eccentric lead of *The Wind Rises*. Almost in real time, we see the suggestion to cast animator and one-time Miyazaki protegé Hideaki Anno grow from throwaway joke to no-brainer decision. We also see how Miyazaki wrestled with the closing moments of the film, and how changing a single word of dialogue at the last minute transformed the emotional climax.

Yet the particulars of production aren't Sunada's top priority. "As I made the film," Sunada told us, "I thought of having a record of what these masters of animation were like in their daily lives as they created their works... portraits of their human qualities – as people, rather than just filmmakers." With that in mind, Sunada manages to draw a remarkably three-dimensional character sketch of Hayao Miyazaki.

The documentary may now be known as fuelling fandom with dozens of grumpy Miyazaki memes, but these candid moments of gravity are mixed with times where the director's demeanour is endearingly avuncular, such as his regular chats with young colleague Sankichi, his "right-hand woman", or when he high-fives staff members after announcing that he has finally finished the film's storyboard. It's a subtly complex view of a complicated and often self-contradictory man, who feels conflicted about the ineffective, "grand hobby" of his career, while displaying models of goats from *Heidi, Girl of the Alps* in front of his private *atelier* workshop for the amusement of local children.

In one final sequence, Miyazaki stands outside the press conference where he's about to announce his retirement. Staring out of the window at the urban landscape, he describes a daring chase sequence that could play out over the rooftops. For the first time in almost two hours, Sunada breaks from her format and presents a montage of scenes from Miyazaki masterpieces: *Lupin III: Castle of Cagliostro, Nausicaä of the Valley of the Wind, Laputa: Castle in the Sky, Spirited Away, Porco Rosso, Princess Mononoke, My Neighbour Totoro, Kiki's Delivery Service* – they're all here. It's a surgical strike to the heartstrings. "When you look from above, so many things reveal themselves to you," Miyazaki says, revealing that spark of genius behind his many beloved films. One that, seemingly, will never fade. "Suddenly, there in your humdrum town is a magical movie."

Above: Long-serving Ghibli producer Toshio Suzuki unwinds in the evening with his acoustic guitar.

Opposite: Mami Sunada's film provides a rare, intimate insight into the working environment at Studio Ghibli.

Isao Takahata and His Tale of the Princess Kaguya

Directed by: Akira Miki, Hidekazu Sato
Length: 85 mins / Year: 2013

....

"I'm not thinking that because it's my last work I have to sum everything up and make this my magnum opus... it just came out this way."

Isao Takahata is very different from Hayao Miyazaki. While the latter flew from one project to the next (until 2023's long-awaited *The Boy and the Heron*), pulling out of retirements and plummeting into productions, Takahata ambled – and in doing so, seemed to make a career-defining masterpiece by mistake.

This film, originally broadcast as two TV episodes in Japan but subsequently paired up as a feature-length

documentary, follows Takahata through the production of what would be his last film, *The Tale of the Princess Kaguya* (2013). Formally, this film's lo-fi production diary style is not particularly invigorating (a similar issue

Opposite: The gorgeous Japanese release poster for the film *The Tale of the Princess Kaguya*.

Below: Director Isao Takahata discusses *Princess Kaguya*, in front of the Japanese promotional poster.

befalls *Never-Ending Man*, see page 156), but there is huge joy to be found in watching Takahata at work, spouting endless wisdom and jokes from his unwavering hearth of a smile.

This is a man lovingly ribbed for being "descended from a giant sloth", and here we fittingly begin proceedings with him curling up on an office sofa, trying to sleep away the production nightmare. It's a gentle, candid moment of everyday life – for him and for the studio. The film is filled with similarly intriguing details that paint (literally in some cases) a picture of the studio at work, like shots of background master Kazuo Oga getting his brushes out, the nubs of worn-down pencils, rows of animators slipping headphones on to work and mundane meetings that could be taking place in any office in the world.

Watching Takahata direct, once suitably power-napped, is fascinating; he is both loose and direct, entirely focused but always ready to adjust. He is "doing battle" with the film, but its making – directed by a man who can't animate and relies on emotional descriptors – is, as the Ghibli staff wearily know, "jotted down". To innovate, in Takahata's case, is to be late. Thanks to a new hand-drawn and CG hybrid production method, deadlines get pushed back to almost comic effect and a rotating door of Ghibli cameos help to shape the figure of Takahata and the production. Producer Yoshiaki Nishimura seems imbued with his director's serenity despite having to become a human stress ball, absorbing crushing pressure but never getting bent out of shape. Composer Joe Hisaishi shows off his musical skills, and his understanding of Takahata's more poetic

directorial style, in an emotional performance that intuits his director's beliefs about the film. The ever-present Toshio Suzuki is passionate but dry, balancing his desire for seeing the film with the task of making it, despite the fact that the standard production facilities of Ghibli "are of no use to [Takahata]".

It is seeing Takahata with his old friend Hayao Miyazaki that is perhaps the most endearing and enduring moment of the film. Miyazaki, working on a shot from *The Wind Rises* (2013), reverts back to being the young man talking to his mentor at Toei Animation, and immediately, excitably, asks for his help – this is Miyazaki at perhaps his most earnest, at least in terms of moments captured on film. The two men beam at

each other, talk shop, joke and discuss birthday plans. When they politely bow goodbye, they wiggle like eager puppies, still buzzing with love. Throughout *Princess Kaguya*'s making, Takahata reveals he is pursuing the realization of "the joy of life" on screen – and in these moments, it can be seen in his own life too.

Above: A feat of feature animation, *The Tale of the Princess Kaguya* is a colourful, visual marvel.

Below: Life Cycle. *The Tale of the Princess Kaguya* follows its title character from her first steps to her symbolic return to the Moon.

Opposite: Isao Takahata and the key cast attend a launch event for The Tale of the Princess Kaguya.

Never-Ending Man: Hayao Miyazaki

Directed by: Kaku Arakawa
Length: 70 mins / Year: 2016

Filmed in the interval between Hayao Miyazaki finishing *The Wind Rises* (2013) and eventually re-entering feature film production with *The Boy and the Heron* (2023), this documentary follows the director as he toys with CGI in the making of the 2018 short film *Boro the Caterpillar*, which would go on to join the library of treasures played at the Ghibli Museum and Ghibli Park cinemas.

Shot in a very matter-of-fact style, this low-budget film (made for TV in Japan) is a simple, fly-on-the-wall capturing of Miyazaki's journey from retiree, to curious hobbyist, to full-time filmmaker. It may be unambitious in its form, but observing Miyazaki in such an unadorned, open manner makes for compelling viewing. Initially, there's great pleasure in just peeking behind the curtain of his atelier to watch the mundanity of a master: making coffee, stoking his fire, feeding birds, doodling

and smoking (even when he's not puffing, another unlit cigarette is always clinging to his bottom lip, waiting). However, once production of *Boro* kicks in, and a CGI team joins the skeleton staff at the Ghibli office, the drama really begins.

Opposite: *Never-Ending Man* is sold on its exclusive access to Hayao Miyazaki as he works.

Below: Hayao Miyazaki provides feedback on the rough animation for the short film *Boro the Caterpillar*.

THE ACADEMY AWARD®-WINNING DIRECTOR OF
SPIRITED AWAY, PRINCESS MONONOKE, AND *MY NEIGHBOR TOTORO*
BEGINS A NEW ADVENTURE

NEVER-ENDING MAN HAYAO MIYAZAKI

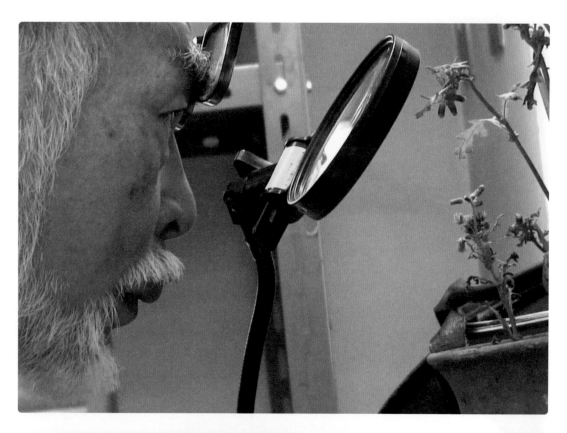

Miyazaki is, perhaps surprisingly, open to the possibilities of the computer, even trying out a tablet to work at, but he's clearly in his element when pencil hits paper. Having held a magnifying glass up to plants to better gauge his flora setting, he starts sketching. "I'm not starting a story yet, that's too limiting," he explains and then hands his hand-drawn character to the CG team. The contrast between the two approaches to animation starts to create great tension, the director exclaiming that the early CG Boro looks like "a new virus". A later, notorious, conversation with an AI-led CG team prompts Miyazaki to call their work an "insult to life itself" and he ultimately ends up being so exacting with his sketches and ideas that the CG team

suggest hand-drawn animation could actually be *quicker* for the production.

It's frustrating that such an interesting period of Ghibli's history is captured in such an amateurish way, with dated, templated title cards, ropey sound and mixing, and no real sense of filmmaking identity (compared to the focused pleasures of 2013's *The Kingdom of Dreams and Madness*). However, the winning footage almost makes up for it.

Apart from the production itself, the most interesting aspect of the film is seeing Miyazaki reckon with his mortality, biologically and professionally. Stalking the halls and desks of his empire, he reveals the deaths of former staff members, both younger than him; he speaks of "devouring" potential successors until he "ate them all"; and he converses with colleagues about the nature of work while standing in front of a wall covered in baby pictures. Life, death and work seem tethered together here, a concept he had already self-consciously explored in *The Wind Rises* and would mine deeper in *The Boy and the Heron*.

Opposite (above): Sketch Artist. Even when toying with using computers to animate *Boro the Caterpillar*, Miyazaki starts with pencils and watercolours.

Opposite (below): To capture the tiny world of insects and bugs in *Boro the Caterpillar*, Miyazaki studies it through a magnifying glass.

Above: Hayao Miyazaki gets to grips with new technology in the making of *Boro the Caterpillar*.

10 Years with Hayao Miyazaki

Directed by: Kaku Arakawa
Length: 196 mins / Year: 2019

Of the Ghibli documentaries that have been made available to global audiences, the four-part miniseries *10 Years with Hayao Miyazaki* has the distinction of being the *most* available.

After its initial television broadcast in 2019, it was released on NHK World's on-demand platform, for free, in a variety of languages. This put it in a perfect position to be discovered by new and hardened fans who, following the landmark streaming deals with Netflix and HBO Max, were diving deep into the Ghibli catalogue, with over three hours of insight and intrigue to satisfy the binger's appetites.

Director Kaku Arakawa has filmed several documentaries about Studio Ghibli and Hayao Miyazaki for TV and home video, with this one sitting in-between the 12-hour-long *How Ponyo Was Born*

(2009) and *Never-Ending Man: Hayao Miyazaki* (2016), which comes in at a more sensible 70 minutes in length. While those two documentaries focused on individual productions, *10 Years with Hayao Miyazaki* culls footage from over a decade of Ghibli history, following Miyazaki during the making of *Ponyo* (2008) and *The Wind Rises* (2013), with interludes focusing on his relationship with his son, Gorō Miyazaki, readying his second feature, *From Up on Poppy Hill* (2011).

Above: Miyazaki may look laid back, but the doc *10 Years with Hayao Miyazaki* captures some of the filmmaker's most conflicted moments.

The first episode, "Ponyo is Here", is the highlight, especially in terms of how it examines the early stages of Miyazaki's creative process, starting from a single drawing of Ponyo which blossoms into a series of non-narrative image boards, before any hint of a screenplay or fixed story.

There seem to be just as many misconceptions about the role and art of the documentary filmmaker as there are for the animated filmmaker, but if you ever want to study the craft of documentary filmmaking, you could compare and contrast this television miniseries with Mami Sunada's *The Kingdom of Dreams and Madness*. The two were made under similar production constraints, with the directors operating their own camera, and they have much of the same access, too, as they were allowed to be close to Hayao Miyazaki as he went about his daily routine while working on his films. They even overlapped in their shooting timelines, as the decade of visits that make up Arakawa's film intersect with Sunada's year-long residence at the studio. Both filmmakers, for example, are present at the production meeting where it is first suggested that Hideaki Anno voice the lead role in *The Wind Rises*, shooting side by side – perhaps piercing the air of intimacy that Sunada carefully created in her film.

Understandably, the presentation of Arakawa's work is more fit for TV broadcast, with many cutaways to clips and archive materials for scene-setting. Yet there's a jarring, intrusive score that feels at odds with the subject. Compared to Sunada, his camerawork is more restless, his framing more journalistic, and his narrative shaping of the edited episodes is much more deliberate: something made most clear in the episode that plays up the intergenerational tensions between Hayao and Gorō Miyazaki, which is titled "Go Ahead – Threaten Me". At times, it feels like something is eluding Arakawa, despite his many years of consistent access and the epic runtime of the finished series.

However, while he may not get under the skin of the studio, he does succeed in capturing possibly the grumpiest Miyazaki moments ever seen in a documentary. Arakawa certainly seems to be a much less tolerated presence than Sunada, who brought out Miyazaki's cheeky, chatty side, but he is also present at times of genuine stress and anguish, such as when the director is struggling with the shadow of *Totoro* as he attempts to return to filmmaking for younger children with *Ponyo*. Whatever the mood, though, Miyazaki is always a fascinating figure to follow.

Going Deeper

If the previous documentaries didn't quench your thirst for insights into the world of Studio Ghibli, you can venture even further – although you'll need to bring along a Japanese phrasebook because they haven't, at time of writing, been officially subtitled in English. But what delights wait for you there if you wade into the depths of Ghibli's documentary catalogue! Love *Princess Mononoke*? There's an exhaustive, 400-minute documentary chronicling its production and release, titled *How Princess Mononoke Was Born* (2001). Can't get enough of Joe Hisaishi? There's the sublime concert film *Joe Hisaishi in Budokan – 25 years with the Animations of Hayao Miyazaki* (2009). Maybe you're an outdoors type? Then turn to the *Scenery of Ghibli* series, which visits the real-life locations that inspired the beautiful natural settings of Ghibli's films and older series such as *Anne of Green Gables* and *Heidi, Girl of the Alps*.

Or perhaps you're curious about the geniuses behind the geniuses? Search out the docs dedicated to art director Kazuo Oga (*A Ghibli Artisan – Kazuo Oga Exhibition – The Man Who Painted Totoro's Forest*, 2007) and influential animator Yasuo Ōtsuka (*Yasuo Ōtsuka's Joy of Motion*, 2004), who was Miyazaki and Takahata's mentor and trusted collaborator in their pre-Ghibli days.

7

Next Ghibli

There will never be another Hayao Miyazaki. And yet, the debate rages on...

If you've reached the end of your Ghibli journey, and wonder what roads to take next, here are a few suggestions. In this chapter, we look at work from filmmakers who have been positioned as "the next Miyazaki" by fans, critics or even by Ghibli itself. They may be former protégés striking out on their own, Ghibli veterans saluting the Studio that they once called home, or distinctive filmmakers in their own right, finding themselves making work that evokes the magic of Miyazaki. The influence and impact of Studio Ghibli are vast, and here we see it across generations of Japanese animation. Some directors struggled with the association, while others beat the old masters at their own game, or chose to rip up the rulebook and forge their own vision for the future of animation.

Nadia: The Secret of Blue Water

Director: Hideaki Anno
Episodes: 39 / Year: 1990

Ever since Hideaki Anno walked into Hayao Miyazaki's office and landed a job as key animator on *Nausicaä of the Valley of the Wind* (1984), the careers of the two men have been intertwined.

In the years since, it is inarguable that Anno has become a legend in his own right, but there is one Miyazaki-flavoured project that plays a key part in his growth as an individual artist. *Nadia: The Secret of Blue Water* sprang from a proposal that Miyazaki pitched to production company Toho in the 1970s: a take on Jules Verne that riffed on the author's landmark science fiction story, *Twenty Thousand Leagues Under the Sea*, and was reportedly titled *Around the World Under the Sea*. The project didn't pan out, but you find glimpses of what could have been across Miyazaki's

work over the ensuing decade in the likes of *Sherlock Hound* (1984) and *Laputa: Castle in the Sky* (1986).

By the end of the 1980s, Toho and broadcaster NHK revisited the idea, and gave the gig to the upstart animation company Gainax, who had by then made their feature debut with *Royal Space Force:*

Opposite: This artwork for *Nadia: The Secret of Blue Water* captures the series' mix of sci-fi and fantasy.

Below: *Nadia* finds director Hideaki Anno discovering his own creative voice, on the cusp of creating his masterwork, *Neon Genesis Evangelion*.

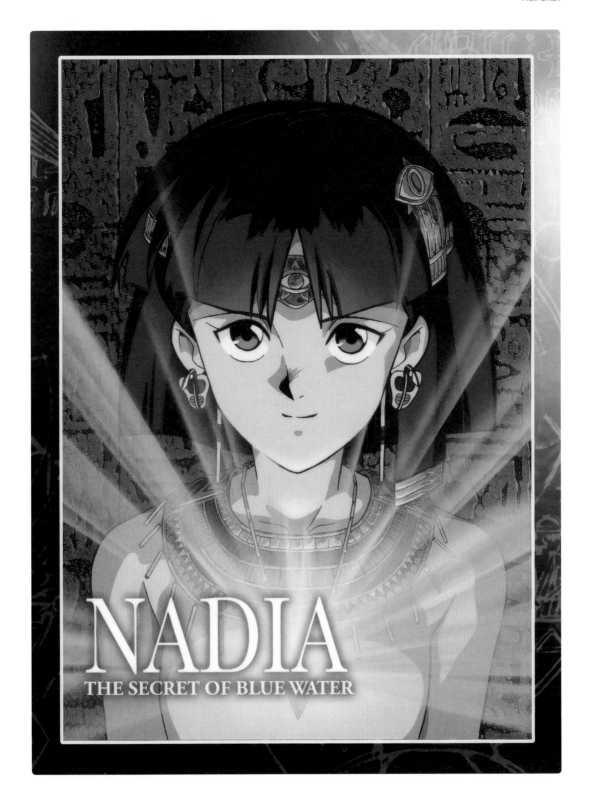

The Wings of Honnêamise (1987) and had enjoyed some commercial success with the OVA series *Gunbuster* (1988). At that point in their history, Gainax were more of a soap opera than a professionally run studio, and there's much drama to dig into behind the scenes, featuring sabre-rattling between creative egos and wildly ambitious (or just plain naive) budgeting for their first television series commission, which left the company's finances in disarray.

In the middle of all that chaos was Hideaki Anno. On Anno's candid "personal biography" on the website for his post-Gainax company, Studio Khara, it's written that it was on *Nadia* that "[Anno] learned firsthand the horrors that lurk within the production of a TV animation series". Some of that chaos can be felt across the span of the series, for instance during a block of 12 episodes made while Anno had to step away from production due to exhaustion, but that didn't stop *Nadia* from becoming a fan favourite, especially in the wider context of Anno's career – one where the fraught, real-life anguish is treated with as much reverence as what happens on screen.

Anno reportedly disliked the scripts that NHK provided for the series, rewriting them himself and moving away from the developed storyline as the episodes progressed, which provides viewers with a fascinating transitional arc that transforms, as we watch, from a highly entertaining Miyazaki tribute to something darker and more distinctively Anno. Early episodes see Nadia and her bespectacled young inventor friend Jean contend with jewel thieves on the streets of turn-of-the-century Paris, before they encounter Captain Nemo and start to investigate the mysteries surrounding the strange crystal that Nadia has in her possession. Then, the real threat emerges: the archvillain Gargoyle and the Neo-Atlanteans who have grand plans of world domination.

These final episodes push *Nadia* into spectacular sci-fi territory, with scenes of explosive battles between hulking space cruisers and flying battleships contrasted with character-led moments of tortured introspection – all pointing the way to Anno's next project, the series that would make his name, *Neon Genesis Evangelion* (1995).

Opposite: Cut-outs of the cast of *Nadia* for the 30th anniversary of the series' original broadcast.

Above: Nadia makes new friends and accomplices, including the Grandis Gang of jewel thieves.

Below: The developing relationship between Nadia and Jean is a thread throughout the series.

Princess Arete

Directed by: Sunao Katabuchi
Length: 105 mins / Year: 2001

....

Sunao Katabuchi was still at university when he started working
with Hayao Miyazaki. Having encountered *Future Boy Conan*
(1978) when he was younger, the film student found himself in
the writer's room for Miyazaki's *Sherlock Hound* (1984–5).

Clearly there must've been some creative sparks
because only a few years later (after some work on
Pacific-hopping, box-office bombing, production *Little
Nemo: Adventures in Slumberland*) he was selected to
direct 1989's *Kiki's Delivery Service*. However, rumour
has it that the funders weren't happy that the film wasn't
under the direction of Miyazaki himself, though being
made at his studio. So, despite wanting a break after the
previous year's *My Neighbour Totoro*, Miyazaki was
back in the director's chair midway through production,
with Katabuchi as assistant director. (This wouldn't be the
only time Miyazaki would take over a production.)

Katabuchi stuck around and helped shepherd new
talent at the studio in the early '90s, but it wouldn't
be until he moved to Studio 4°C (*Memories, Mind
Game, Tekkonkinkreet*) that Katabuchi would get to
make his feature debut, 2001's *Princess Arete*, a project
developed by the filmmaker with a trusted colleague:
his wife, Chie Uratani. Working with her husband
as either animation director or assistant director
(including on 2016's *In This Corner of the World*, the
acclaimed, crowd-funded and stunning animated
wartime drama), Uratani is "in charge of the drawings",
Katabuchi explained to Anime World News, saying
his "inspirations come from trying to figure out what
inspires [his] wife's animation".

The story is about a lonely princess, trapped in a
gilded royal life – and tower. She's so curious about
the workings of life, from glass-blowing to darning
socks, that she sneaks out of her castle at every
opportunity to be among the working townspeople.
After various men try to ensnare her hand in marriage
by presenting colonially pillaged supernatural objects,
she ends up moving from one cage to another. As a
result of some literal trickery, she is betrothed to an evil
wizard and becomes a trinket in his even lonelier tower,
from which she must find a way to escape.

Adapted from Diana Coles's English-language novel
The Clever Princess (1983), there are clear Ghibli fibres
in the film, from the broader strokes of its narrative to the
finer details. The art style, featuring small facial features,
fine outlines and an autumnal palette, feels more
European compared to the more common "anime"
look. Within this look the Princess's curiosity and
adoration for everyday life and craft are reflected in
patient detail, which makes her later isolation that much
more painful. But through her ingenuity, pragmatism
and ultimately feminist beliefs, she's able to overturn
evil, outrun patriarchy and find independence (she'd
definitely be pals with Kiki). Arete's story is charmed
with fairy tale familiarity and moves at a slow pace,
allowing the animation to quietly observe the world and
emotionally persevere with Arete. The resulting slow
rhythm may be frustrating for some, but is essential for
the film's empathetic realization of loneliness that would
elude a breezier, bed-time version.

In This Corner of the World would later win Katabuchi
the top spot on the prestigious Kinema Jumpo Film of
the Year list – the only other animated film to win it?
My Neighbour Totoro – but his first feature is a must
to make time for. Beautiful, meditative and refreshing,
Princess Arete shows a filmmaker shaped within, but
now thrillingly outside, the palace gates of Ghibli.

Opposite: The Japanese poster for *Princess Arete*, featuring an
evocative, colourful sketch of our heroine.

Children Who Chase Lost Voices

Directed by: Makoto Shinkai
Length: 116 mins / Year: 2011

With Makoto Shinkai, in terms of how he became more widely considered a Miyazaki successor, it's less about form and more about finance.

His 2016 meteoric hit *Your Name* briefly overtook *Spirited Away* (2001) at the all-time box office in Japan – he had knocked the king from his perch... until *Spirited Away* was rereleased in cinemas and took back its place. His following films *Weathering With You* (2019) and *Suzume* (2022) completed a trilogy of character studies packaged in disaster films, all relishing in hyper-detailed animation, rollicking speed-rock scores and teen melodrama, the latter two being box office smashes as well. Here was a man with a distinctly cinematic vision creating standalone animated

stories with an unmistakable style and scoring big at the box office. Very Miyazaki.

But those recent successes aren't particularly Miyazaki-esque in their style; they're full of sharp, urban surfaces, cell-phone mannerisms and maxed-out emotion. The closest Miyazaki came to those Shinkai

Below: Two young lovers framed by a breathtaking vista. A familiar sight in a Makoto Shinkai film.

Opposite: Shinkai's films are sumptuous, as seen on the cover of this official companion book.

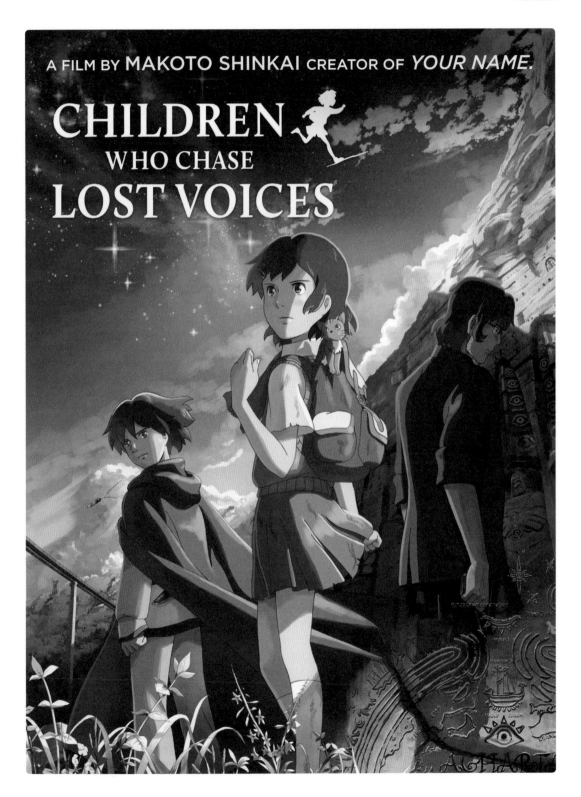

films is perhaps in scripting the teen dalliance of 1995's *Whisper of the Heart*. Look back to 2011, however, before Shinkai was a global name in animation, and you'll find *Children Who Chase Lost Voices*. By no means a Miyazaki-level hit, but one totally indebted to him, this is a film that shows the breadth of Shinkai's creativity.

Taking place on the fringes of town and country, the story begins with Asuna, a young girl, whose father has died, and who finds solace and solitude at the edge of a forest, listening to mysterious, other-worldly radio broadcasts. A brief, and ultimately tragic, interaction with magical boy Shun starts Asuna on a journey inside her grief, and the core of Planet Earth, in search of the dead. Journeying with her is her teacher Ryūji – a similarly grief-stricken character, who joins the quest by nefarious, militaristic means – and Shun's younger brother Shin, the trio bound together on an odyssey into Agartha, a fantasy kingdom in the hollow

earth. Although the narrative goes to unusual places, melancholy travels through every one of the film's rich locations, carried by Asuna, Ryūji and Shin, who long for parents, spouses and siblings.

As the story descends through planes of planetary existence, Shinkai's typical sleek urban settings disappear, allowing the director famed for his sharpened realities to explore the exact opposite, revealing an expressionistic and surrealist image-maker. Agartha is an alchemic sandbox of myth and legend for Shinkai, where references to figures of Greek myth-like Orpheus and Eurydice are collided with Aztec-inspired gods, and biblical, Lovecraftian all-seeing angelic monsters. The cool tones of metal and glass give way to bright swathes of blooming nature and gooey, harshly etched, devilish figures. This is a world where each new scene is an opportunity to surprise, shock and delight with character invention and action – best illustrated by the moment when a nude,

one-armed giant swallows our heroes whole and proceeds to jump off a cliff.

Outside of the central story, there is some condensed, messy world building – like trying to jam all of *The Lord of the Rings* into two hours – something that is avoided by more revered fantasy adventures like Miyazaki's *Princess Mononoke* (1997) or *Laputa: Castle in the Sky* (1986). While Shinkai's film tries to explain the details of his world, Miyazaki's are the reverse, in that they allow the details to explain the world. Those films are teasing, unfinished maps, rather than encyclopedias. Although *Children* lacks the narrative elegance of some Ghibli works, it's full of thematic and visual familiarity that shows where Shinkai was studying ahead of his fantastical foray. Characters fall while clutching exploding precious gems as in *Castle in the Sky*; regular, detailed, insert shots of bugs and creatures could come from *My Neighbour Totoro* (1988); and Mimi, Asuna's fox-like feline companion, could be a

descendent of Nausicaä's sharp-toothed Teto (or of the ones that inhabit Laputa). Sprinkle in some delicately prepared family meals, some satisfying cleaning and even a moment to lie down on some green grass against a bright blue sky, and if you squint a bit, the land of Agartha could be another destination where Howl's castle travels to explore. There is a respect and curiosity for nature and spirituality, and how the two entwine, as well as some superbly strange design that showcases a very different filmmaker to the one who went stratospheric with *Your Name*. Although unwieldy and surreal, Shinkai's world here has a very human emotional core, the famed hyperrealist finding reality in the bizarre.

Opposite: With this adventure, Makoto Shinkai found himself in Miyazaki territory, with familiar sights like magical crystals...

Below: ...and fantastical flying machines, recalling the likes of *Laputa: Castle in the Sky* – the first film the director paid to see with his own pocket money.

A Letter to Momo

Directed by: Hiroyuki Okiura
Length: 120 mins / Year: 2011

....

A Letter to Momo is perhaps a surprising left turn from director Hiroyuki Okiura, a star animator who excelled for decades in the realm of sci-fi animation with the likes of *Akira* (1988), *Patlabor 2: The Movie* (1993), *Ghost in the Shell* (1995) and *Memories* (1995).

Across those works, he had built a reputation as one of anime's foremost exponents of a style of animation that was detailed almost to the point of photorealism. In an interview with the indispensable animation blog *Full Frontal*, frequent collaborator Toshiyuki Inoue once described Okiura's approach as following the maxims "high precision" and "accuracy without any lies".

Okiura's directorial debut, *Jin-Roh: The Wolf Brigade* (1999), was a dark, dystopian melodrama, but his second feature is a whimsical mixture of human drama and Japanese folklore which found the filmmaker courting comparisons with the work of Hayao Miyazaki. *A Letter to Momo* tells the story of a young woman who moves from Tokyo to a small island in the Seto Inland Sea following the death of her father. There, in her mother's childhood hometown, she meets three cheeky *yōkai* creatures who cause havoc with the locals, before helping her to work through her grief and reconnect with the world.

Seriously, if you had a penny for every use of terms such as "Ghibli-esque" or "Miyazaki-like" in the coverage of the film from English-language media, you'd be set for life. Critics couldn't help themselves from pointing out themes and settings that recalled the likes of *My Neighbour Totoro* or *Spirited Away*. Allegra Frank at *Film Comment* positioned the film as a prime example of "post-Miyazaki" anime, while the *Hollywood Reporter* noted that it "could easily pass for a new Studio Ghibli release".

Perhaps that wasn't so surprising, though. While Okiura's career had never led him to Studio Ghibli, many of his key collaborators on the film were Ghibli

Above: This promotional artwork for *A Letter to Momo* shows our lead character flanked by the supernatural tricksters, the yōkai.

Opposite: Like the best Miyazaki films, *A Letter to Momo* juxtaposes the everyday and the otherworldly.

veterans, including animation director and character designer Masashi Ando (who performed the same roles on both *Princess Mononoke* and *Spirited Away*), as well as Hiroyuki Morita (director of *The Cat Returns*), Takeshi Honda and Toshiyuki Inoue. Many of these animators were schooled in the Ghibli house style, but here they were working without the exacting hand of Hayao Miyazaki.

That makes *A Letter to Momo* a fascinating example of a film that feels "post-Miyazaki", but its relationship with Ghibli doesn't stop there. Following the release of the film, Okiura did eventually find himself contributing to a Ghibli feature, *When Marnie Was There* (2014), which was touted as the first Ghibli project that didn't have direct involvement from the older generation, with Hiromasa Yonebayashi in the director's chair and Masashi Ando once again fulfilling the role of animation director and character designer. And

then, when it came time for Miyazaki to return from retirement once more for *The Boy and the Heron* (2023), his advanced age led him to delegate more than ever to his animation team, which shared many names with the Momo crew, not least Takeshi Honda, who had been promoted to animation director.

A final word to the wise: while *A Letter to Momo* is indeed a mature, heart-warming film, the same cannot be said for Okiura's sole directorial credit in the years since. *Robot on the Road* (2015) is a gorgeously animated but unbelievably juvenile short film that follows the exploits of a degenerate robot hitchhiker as he attempts to take candid pictures of the unsuspecting young woman who gives him a lift. Many members of Momo's animation team returned for the project, contributing extraordinary character work – but the tasteless content is perhaps not the best application of their talents.

Wolf Children

Directed by: Mamoru Hosoda
Length: 117 mins / Year: 2012

Mamoru Hosoda is one of the great depictors of the internet age.

From his mid-length debut *Digimon Adventure: Our War Game!* (2000), which connected the monsters of a franchise with the monstrosities of a cyber security threat, to *Summer Wars* (2009) which combined meeting the in-laws with a global web-based apocalypse, to fairy tale remix *Belle* (2021) which put *Beauty and the Beast* into the metaverse, he's a director who has consistently understood the evolving language of the internet across two decades of storytelling. Compared to Hosoda, Studio Ghibli isn't exactly known for embracing IT in their stories, instead revering nature, spirituality and tradition over computers. It's strange to think, then, that Mamoru Hosoda was at one point going to be the future of Ghibli.

He had seen and loved *Lupin III: The Castle of Cagliostro* (1979) when he was 12 and his favourite TV anime was Takahata's *Anne of Green Gables* (1979). Since viewing them he had been "obsessed with animation and making animation", so after the success of *Digimon*, when Ghibli offered him the chance to direct *Howl's Moving Castle* (2004), he was almost circling back to where his passion began. As we know, he never made that film and the full details of why remain elusive, but he did later tell Polygon: "If I had to make *Howl's* the way Ghibli wanted me to make it, I think my career would have been over ... when I got off the project, people thought, 'Oh, he failed, he's over.' But it's a good thing that I went on to make my own thing, instead of making it the way Miyazaki would have made it."

So Miyazaki made *Howl's Moving Castle* and Hosoda would break out with the temporal-looping adventure *The Girl Who Leapt Through Time* in 2006, followed by *Summer Wars* three years later. He had admired Ghibli, worked with them and left

them, and then when launching his own fledgling studio, Studio Chizu, Hosoda decided to make (what remains) his most Ghibli film: *Wolf Children*. It's the story of a woman who falls in love with a wolfman, bears his similarly lupine-souled children and, after a tragedy, has to raise them solo, in a new house in the countryside. An exploration of identity, as much for the mother as it is the children, it touches on the divide between city and country, human and nature, the mundane and the fantastical, all observed with a keen eye for the details of our environment and the foibles of humanity. As with other Hosoda works, and most egregiously in *The Boy and the Beast* (2015), the filmmaker can't resist pushing the narrative into a destructive finale, in this case a large flood (something, ironically, Miyazaki handles with more grace and reasoning in 2008's *Ponyo*). It shows a lack of confidence in his actually quite sharp character work, forcing melodrama on them to provoke emotion, rather than letting it grow organically from them. Although it ends rather disappointingly, *Wolf Children* does show that if he had stuck around, and been offered the right guidance, Mamoru Hosoda might have made a high-ranking Ghibli film. But it's more exciting that he didn't, because outside of the confines of Ghibli, Hosoda would go on to become one of the most distinct, most exciting animation directors in the world.

Opposite: *Wolf Children* is Mamoru Hosoda's tribute to mothers and the trials of parenthood.

Mary and the Witch's Flower

Directed by: Hiromasa Yonebayashi
Length: 103 mins / Year: 2017

The saying goes that "imitation is the sincerest form of flattery", and they don't come more sincere than *Mary and the Witch's Flower*. For one feature, Studio Ponoc performed as the world's greatest Studio Ghibli Tribute Act.

However, this is far from the Bootleg Beatles. Perhaps a better analogy would be to say that this was an ace backing band stepping into the limelight after the frontman had left the stage.

Ponoc was created by a younger generation left in the lurch by Ghibli's surprise shuttering following the release of *The Wind Rises* (2013), *The Tale of the Princess Kaguya* (2013) and *When Marnie Was There* (2014), aiming to preserve the studio's dedication to high-quality feature animation that entertains kids and

grown-ups alike. Studio founder Yoshiaki Nishimura was the producer of the latter two films, and he took with him director Hiromasa Yonebayashi, fresh off *Marnie*, and an all-star team of Ghibli veterans, including animation director Takeshi Inamura, assistant

Opposite: Packed with familiar sights, *Mary and the Witch's Flower* is a fitting tribute to the films of Ghibli.

Below: Mary fits seamlessly into Ghibli's line of female protagonists, such as Kiki, Chihiro and Arrietty.

animation director Ei Inoue, and key animators such as Masashi Ando, Akihiko Yamashita and Shinji Otsuka – all of whom would eventually end up back at Ghibli again, working on *The Boy and the Heron* (2023).

There's something delightfully uncanny about *Mary and the Witch's Flower*. Every step of the way, Ponoc seems to be following a recipe for a Ghibli adventure at its most spellbinding. A whimsical, English-language source novel? Check. A humdrum everyday world enlivened by magic? Check. A girl on a broom, a boy on a bike and a black cat companion? Check, check, check. But Mary isn't Kiki, as much as the plot keywords and flourishes in the animation may suggest. Mary Stewart's source novel, *The Little Broomstick*, is far more strange, even psychedelic. After all, Mary's first experience of magic comes after being exposed to a curious, trippy flower, and elsewhere inspiration is drawn from the darker corners of religion and history, ranging from the name of the magic school Mary is whisked away to, Endor College (referring to the Biblical Witch of Endor), to the name of one of its teachers, Dr Dee, a nod to Elizabethan scientist and occultist John Dee.

Ponoc's adaptation is full to the brim with magical ideas, distinctive character designs and bravura sequences of animation that recall the giddy heights of Ghibli films past. The lush landscapes of the recognizably British setting evoke the trademark green hills and blue skies seen in many a Ghibli classic, while the surplus of spells and experiments found within Endor College recall the overflowing imagination and countless creatures of *Spirited Away*'s bathhouse. Indeed, the very design of the College, an island floating aloft above the clouds, recalls *Laputa: Castle in the Sky*. Yet there's a yearning at the heart of the story, as Mary discovers not just magic but a magical legacy, and a family history along with it, which sees Nishimura and Yonebayashi returning to the thematic thread they started themselves on *When Marnie Was There* – sneaking a song of their own into the greatest hits set list.

Right: For more magical fantasy from author Mary Stewart, check out her trilogy of novels recounting Arthurian legends from the perspective of Merlin.

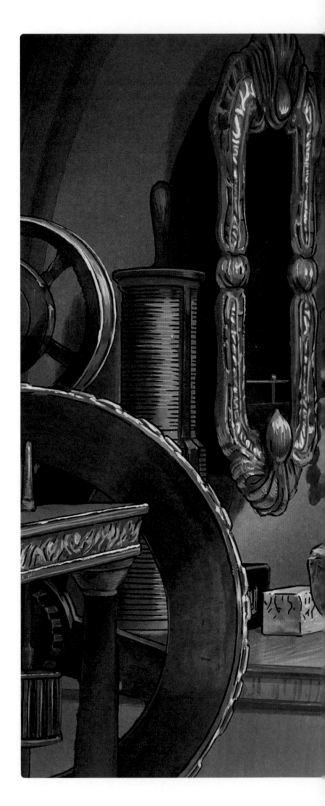

Lu Over the Wall

Directed by: Masaaki Yuasa
Length: 112 mins / Year: 2017

Diving into a Masaaki Yuasa project is always an invigorating and surprising experience.

His 2004 feature debut *Mind Game* featured a conversation between man and God, the deity represented as a form-shifting personification of animation itself; his 2021 globally acclaimed release *Inu-Oh* combined historical epic and rock opera; and his 2020 series *Keep Your Hands Off Eizouken!* examined and championed the making of animation, via a small anime club led by loveable teenage fans (their fandom kickstarted by a viewing of Miyazaki's *Future Boy Conan*). A prolific storyteller, working in serialized and standalone stories, Yuasa released two films in 2017: *Lu Over the Wall* and the romance *Night Is Short, Walk On Girl*, which although fantastic, doesn't feature as much Ghibli DNA (or character cameos) as *Lu*.

Set in a small seaside town, *Lu Over the Wall* is the story of Kai, a lonely, awkward, musically minded boy who strikes up a friendship with two fellow musicians – and a mermaid (or ningyo). Although he is older, and more insular than *Ponyo*'s leading lad Sōsuke, his adventure is not dissimilar to the *Little Mermaid* riff that Hayao Miyazaki played in 2008. When Kai is with his band on the mystical and dangerous "merfolk island", the sounds ripple through the waves, infecting half-human, half-fish Lu with so much groove that her single fin splits into two dizzying, dancing feet, and she soon joins the group. With her rubbery transformation, and even her frog-like face, Lu could certainly be a relative of Ponyo, and considering she also eventually gets embroiled in a sublime coastal flood, you could say they have similar pastimes too.

Yuasa is very much aware of the connection between his film and Miyazaki's, drawing attention to their similarities in varying levels of subtlety. During

a particularly wet sequence, 'Ride of the Valkyries' is included in the musical score – a piece that joyfully contradicted a wave-hopping routine in *Ponyo* – and a more direct example is when the recognizable undercut of *Ponyo*'s Sosuke and mum Lisa are seen in the flood (a flood that was also inspired by Isao Takahata's

Above: Director Masaaki Yuasa poses with a toy version of the mermaid star of his film, *Lu Over the Wall*.

Opposite: This artwork for *Lu Over the Wall* shows off the strange, near-psychedelic style of the film.

Panda! Go Panda!: Rainy Day Circus, explored on page 17). It's not all hat tips and Ghibli reverence with *Lu*, though: the eccentric, flexible sensibilities of Yuasa led to a showcase of a broad range of influences, especially during the film's musical sequences which shimmy through the psychedelia of *Yellow Submarine* (1968) via the satisfying concentricities of Busby Berkeley and even Jacques Demy's arthouse sob-along *The Umbrellas of Cherbourg* (1964). With the addition of fantastic character designs, not limited to a giant walking shark, a troupe of fish skeletons and a team of mer-dogs, it's hard to keep pace with the invention on screen.

Despite wearing its inspirations clearly on its wetsuit sleeve, *Lu* is still unmistakably Yuasa's film because it is his dexterity, and his willingness to experiment and fluctuate in form, that makes him so intriguing and exciting as a director. While one scene feels like watching sprays of water light up and dance like a laser show in a planetarium, another feels like a child's drawing plucked from the door of a refrigerator and thrust into animated life. For many viewers, discovering Yuasa's work can be a transformative experience, and in his animation, so often, transformation is what makes the experience so special as well.

Above: One of the film's more bizarre flourishes is Lu's grinning, thinly-disguised shark father.

Right: Awkward teenager Kai finds himself in uncharted waters when he meets the magical, music-loving mermaid, Lu.

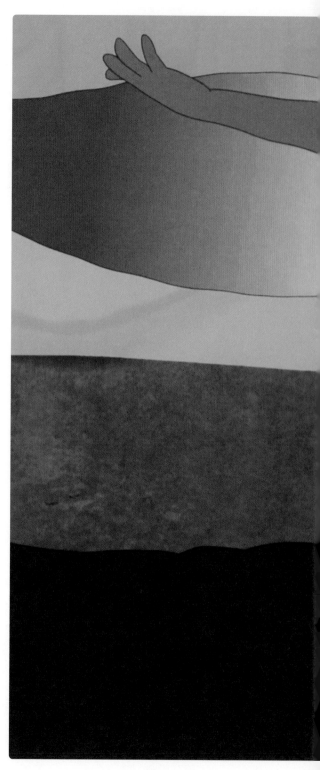

The Deer King

Directed by: Masashi Ando, Masayuki Miyaji
Length: 113 mins / Year: 2021

The Deer King (2021) is an adventure story that has as much an eye on agriculture as it does on artillery and sees characters navigating war, disease and gloopy, violent monsters in a perhaps futile quest for peace.

In other words, it's probably going to feel quite familiar if you like Ghibli films, especially *Princess Mononoke* (1997). And, with a quick glance at the résumés of directors Masashi Ando and Masayuki Miyaji, it's not hard to see why they were selected to direct this fantasy tale. Ando worked as a key animator on the likes of *Porco Rosso* (1992), *Princess Mononoke* and *My Neighbours the Yamadas* (1999), and outside of Ghibli he worked with visionary storytellers like Satoshi Kon (*Paprika*), Hideaki Anno (*Evangelion: 3.0 You Can (Not) Redo*) and Makoto Shinkai (*Your Name*) and in 2017 he even worked with Studio Ponoc on their Ghibli tribute film *Mary and the Witch's Flower*. Miyaji,

unlike Ando, doesn't have a huge number of Ghibli credits to his name, but he did work incredibly close to the master, acting as assistant director on Hayao Miyazaki's 2001 film *Spirited Away* and *Mei and the Baby Cat Bus*, a short sequel to *My Neighbour Totoro*, which is exclusively shown at the Ghibli Park and Ghibli Museum (see page 54 for more details).

The Deer King began life as a novel by Nahoko Uehashi published in 2014. It then became a manga series, and finally a film, produced by Production

Below: With his cursed arm wound and horned animal companion, Van bears semblance to Ashitaka, the male lead of *Princess Mononoke*.

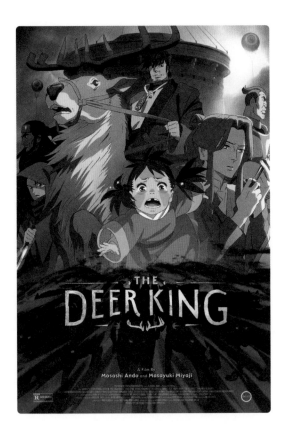

I.G., whose previous animated features include *Ghost in the Shell* (1995), *Jin-Roh: The Wolf Brigade* (2000) and this chapter's *A Letter to Momo* (2011). Set in a magical, medievally fashioned territory, the story follows Van, an imprisoned convict, whose jail is attacked by a pack of poisonous dogs. The dogs ravage the place, leaving Van with a cursed bite mark on his arm (very Ashitaka) and a new calling, to look after the only other survivor, a young orphan called Yuna. Yuna and Van begin a life that's quaint and charming; gruff and innocent, together they toil the land and revel in its simple beauty. It's in its exploration and representation of nature that *The Deer King* is at its strongest, lyrically binding imagery via match cuts – like breastfeeding to milking cows or tree branches to fingertips – to underpin the similarities and co-dependent relationship between humanity and its environment. These details are painted in gleaming light and precise detail, showing the care taken by not just the animator's hand but by the characters too. Here nature is cherished. It's this approach that makes

the inevitable destruction all the more powerful, and once war comes to Yuna and Van, it ravages the grace of their surroundings in wincing fashion. This vague war doesn't just destroy the beauty in those moments, though; unfortunately, it goes on to diminish the film's story as well. Large chunks of *The Deer King* are dedicated to talking through grinding bureaucracy, which makes for tedious viewing, leaving the events of the film perhaps thoroughly explained but not satisfyingly told. Unlike the thrilling moral complexity that *Princess Mononoke* offers viewers, the complexities here become complications, which in turn creates tedium. A subplot about a virus and the discovery of its cure (the film itself was delayed due to the COVID-19 pandemic) makes for timely, and more gripping, viewing than the film's parliamentary discussions, but *The Deer King* is at its best with its central duo and their outdoor excursions. Philosophically and stylistically, Ghibli fans will certainly find an ally in *The Deer King*, but in terms of breaking new ground? It ends up in no man's land.

Top: An action-packed poster for *The Deer King* from its North American release via distributor GKIDS.

Above: For all its lore and political intrigue, *The Deer King* is at its best when it's depicting natural beauty.

Further Reading and Watching

In addition to the invaluable books and articles listed below, we would like to thank GKIDS, StudioCanal, Anime Ltd and Elysian Films for providing press materials that helped us explore the Ghibliverse. As with our previous book, *Ghibliotheque*, we also drew from over a decade of personal research, including two trips to Japan and interviews with Isao Takahata, Toshio Suzuki, Gorō Miyazaki, Mami Sunada, Makoto Shinkai, Mamoru Hosoda, Hiromasa Yonebayashi, Yoshiaki Nishimura, Steve Alpert, Rebecca Sugar, Enrico Casarosa, Alex Dudok de Wit, Tom Morton-Smith and Basil Twist.

Books

Alpert, Steve, *Sharing a House with the Never-Ending Man* (Berkeley, Stone Bridge Press, 2020)

Clements, Jonathan & McCarthy, Helen, *The Anime Encyclopedia*, 3rd rev. ed. (Berkeley, Stone Bridge Press, 2015)

Clements, Jonathan & Osmond, Andrew, *Future Boy Conan: Miyazaki's Directorial Debut* (Glasgow, Anime Ltd, 2021)

Denison, Rayna, *Studio Ghibli: An Industrial History* (New York, Springer International Publishing, 2023)

Denison, Rayna (ed.), *Princess Mononoke: Understanding Studio Ghibli's Monster Princess* (London, Bloomsbury Academic, 2018)

Dudok de Wit, Alex, *BFI Film Classics: Grave of the Fireflies* (London, Bloomsbury Publishing, 2021)

Ghibli Museum, Mitaka (The Tokuma Memorial Cultural Foundation for Animation, 2010)

Ghibli Park: Official Guide Book (Ghibli Park Co., Ltd, 2022)

Ghibli Roman Album: Conan, the Boy in Future (Tokyo, Tokuma Shoten, 2003)

Ghibli Warehouse: Official Pamphlet (Ghibli Park Co., Ltd, 2022)

Hara, Kunio, *33¹/³ Japan: My Neighbor Totoro Soundtrack* (London, Bloomsbury Academic, 2020)

Kadono, Eiko, *Kiki's Delivery Service*, translated by Emily Balistrieri (Penguin Random House Children's, 2020)

Kelts, Roland (ed.) *Essays on Grave of the Fireflies* (New York, Anime: Masters & Masterpieces, 2008)

Le Guin, Ursula K. *The Books of Earthsea* (London, Gollancz, 2018)

McCarthy, Helen, *Hayao Miyazaki: Master of Japanese Animation* (Berkeley, Stone Bridge Press, 1999)

Miyazaki, Hayao, *Nausicaä of the Valley of the Wind*, box set (San Francisco, VIZ Media, 2012)

Miyazaki, Hayao, *Shuna's Journey*, translated by Alex Dudok de Wit (New York, First Second Books, 2022)

Miyazaki, Hayao, *Starting Point: 1979–1996*, translated by Beth Cary and Frederik L. Schodt (San Francisco, VIZ Media, 2009)

Miyazaki, Hayao, *Turning Point: 1997–2008*, translated by Beth Cary and Frederik L. Schodt (San Francisco, VIZ Media, 2014)

Miyazawa, Kenji, *Night Train to the Stars*, translated by John Bester (London, Vintage Classics, 2022)

Napier, Susan, *Miyazakiworld: A Life in Art* (London, Yale University Press, 2018)

Niebel, Jessica, *Hayao Miyazaki* (Los Angeles, Academy Museum of Motion Pictures, 2021)

Norton, Mary, *The Borrowers Anthology* (London, JM Dent and Sons, 1966)

Odell, Colin & Le Blanc, Michelle, *Studio Ghibli: The Films of Hayao Miyazaki and Isao Takahata* (Harpenden, Hertfordshire, Kamera Books, 2009)

Osmond, Andrew, *BFI Film Classics: Spirited Away* (London, Bloomsbury Publishing, 2008)

Robinson, Joan G., *When Marnie Was There* (London, HarperCollins, 2014)

Royal Shakespeare Company, *My Neighbour Totoro* (show programme, 2022)

Studio Ghibli, *Hayao Miyazaki and the Ghibli Museum* (Tokyo, Iwanami Shoten, 2021)

Studio Ghibli, *Studio Ghibli: The Complete Works* (New York, Vertical, 2022)

Suzuki, Toshio, *Mixing Work with Pleasure: My Life at Studio Ghibli*, translated by Roger Speares (Tokyo, Japan Publishing Industry Foundation for Culture, 2018)

Thomas Smith, Karl, *Now Go: Grief and Studio Ghibli* (Edinburgh, 404 Ink, 2022)

Wynne Jones, Diana, *Earwig and the Witch* (London, HarperCollins Children's Books, 2011)

Wynne Jones, Diana, *Howl's Moving Castle* (London, HarperCollins Children's Books, 2009)

Yoshino, Genzaburo, *How Do You Live?*, translated by Bruno Navasky (London, Rider, 2021)

Articles, interviews and blogs

'Hideaki Anno confesses episodes from his time as director of "Aim for the Top!" & "Nadia: The Secret of the Sea"!', Cinema Café, 2014. https://www.cinemacafe.net/article/2014/10/28/26930.html

'Iwata Asks, Volume 8: Yoichi Kotabe: The Search for Greater Creativity'. https://web.archive.org/web/20130613050241/https://iwataasks.nintendo.com/interviews/#/ds/dsi/7/1

Alderdice, Kit. 'Q&A with Diana Wynne Jones', Publisher's Weekly, 2008. https://www.publishersweekly.com/pw/by-topic/authors/interviews/article/5902-q-a-with-diana-wynne-jones.html.

Dockery, Daniel, 'Spirited Away Stage Director Discusses Meeting Miyazaki and Adapting a Classic Anime Film', Crunchyroll News, April 17, 2023. https://www.crunchyroll.com/news/interviews/2023/4/17/interview-spirited-away-stage-director-discusses-meeting-miyazaki-and-adapting-a-classic-anime-film

Frank, Allegra, 'Getting fired from a Miyazaki movie was "a good thing" for this anime director', Polygon, October 20, 2018. https://www.polygon.com/2018/10/20/18001588/mamoru-hosoda-fired-howls-moving-castle-interview

Horn, Carl Gustav, 'The Conscience of the Otaking: The Studio Gainax Saga in Four Parts', Animerica, 4 (2), (1996). Available at:https://gwern.net/doc/anime/eva/1996-animerica-conscience#part-4

Inoa, Christopher L, 'How the Chaos of Making Nadia: The Secret of Blue Water Almost Killed an Anime Studio', IGN Southeast Asia, August 6, 2022. https://sea.ign.com/nadia-the-secret-of-blue-water/188752/feature/how-the-chaos-of-making-nadia-the-secret-of-blue-water-almost-killed-an-anime-studio

Iwabuchi, Deborah, 'How Do You Live? An Interview with Translator Bruno Navasky', SCBWI Japan Translation Group, February 2, 2022. https://ihatov.wordpress.com/2022/02/02/how-do-you-live-an-interview-with-bruno-navasky/

Le Guin, Ursula K, 'Tales from Earthsea or Gedo Senki' (Studio Ghibli, 2006). https://www.ursulakleguin.com/adaptation-tales-of-earthsea

Martin, Elyse, 'The Magic of Translation: Interviewing Kiki's Delivery Service Author Eiko Kadono and Translator Emily Balistrieri', Tor.com, August 6, 2020. https://www.tor.com/2020/08/06/the-magic-of-translation-interviewing-kikis-delivery-service-author-eiko-kadono-and-translator-emily-balistrieri/

Meyer, Joshua, 'Spirited Away: Live On Stage Director John Caird On Achieving The Impossible', Slashfilm.com, April 17, 2023. https://www.slashfilm.com/1253182/spirited-away-live-on-stage-director-exclusive-interview/

Miller, Bob, 'The Secrets of Howl's Moving Castle', Starlog, August 2005, pp. 36–40. Available at: https://scrapsfromtheloft.com/movies/the-secrets-of-howls-moving-castle-by-bob-miller/

Mukhtar, Amel, 'Mei Mac Recreates Anime Magic On The Barbican Stage In My Neighbour Totoro', British Vogue, November 19, 2002. https://www.vogue.co.uk/arts-and-lifestyle/article/mei-mac-interview

Nakajima, Junzō, 'The schedule was tough, but this work was blessed with good luck', Ghibli Museum, 2010. https://www.ghibli-museum.jp/anne/kataru/nakajima/

Nguyen, Hanh, 'Studio Ghibli's Miyazaki — No, the Other One — On Inheriting His Father's Legacy with "Ronja, the Robber's Daughter"', Indiewire, February 2, 2017. https://www.indiewire.com/features/general/ronja-the-robbers-daughter-goro-miyazaki-studio-ghibli-animation-1201777087/

Peters, Megan, 'Spirited Away: Live on Stage Interview: Director John Caird on Ghibli's Legacy and Puppet Wrangling', Comicbook.com, April 24, 2023.. https://comicbook.com/anime/news/studio-ghibli-movie-spirited-away-play-interview/

Phillips, Jevon, 'Goro Miyazaki helps guide "Ronja, the Robber's Daughter" to Amazon', Los Angeles Times, February 22, 2017. https://www.latimes.com/entertainment/herocomplex/la-et-st-goro-miyazaki-ronja-robbers-20170222-story.html

Robinson, Tasha, 'Spirited Away's stage director says Hayao Miyazaki is a sweetheart — and a songwriter', Polygon, April 20, 2023. https://www.polygon.com/23689921/spirited-away-live-on-stage-director-interview-john-caird

Takahata, Isao, 'When I Heard about the Release, I Was Surprised at First, but Now I'm Happy I Was Asked to Do It'. Ghibli Museum, 2010. https://www.ghibli-museum.jp/anne/kataru/takahata/

Watzky, Matteo, 'World Masterpiece Theater Production History', Animétudes, 2021-2022. https://animetudes.com/category/series/world-masterpiece-theater-production-history/

Index

Picture Credits

....

The publishers would like to thank the following sources for their kind permission to reproduce the pictures in this book.

Key: p = page, t = top, l = left, r = right, b = bottom, tl = top left, tr = top right, bl = bottom left, br = bottom right, cr = centre right.

p4 STUDIO GHIBLI / Album / Newscom; p6bl & br Album / Alamy Stock Photo; p7tl Associated Press / Alamy Stock Photo; p7tr TOKUMA SHOTEN / Album / Newscom; p8-9 Photo by Jeremie Souteyrat / Figarophoto / Camera Press, London; p10 Miles Gowar; p11 Henry St John / Shutterstock; p12, p15 Photo 12 / Alamy Stock Photo; p16 Tokyo Movie Shinsha; p17, p18 TMS All Rights Reserved; p19 Allstar Picture Library Limited / Alamy Stock Photo; p20 Newscom / Alamy Stock Photo; p21 Kyodo / Newscom; p22 Genoa Edition / Nippon Animation Co Ltd; p23, p25, p26, p27, p28, p29, p30 Nippon Animation Co Ltd; p32, p33, p34 Original Comic Books Created by Monkey Punch All Rights Reserved / TMS All Rights Reserved; p37, p38, p39 Photo 12 / Alamy Stock Photo; p40 TMS All Rights Reserved; p41tl, p41tr, p42-43 TMS All Rights Reserved; p44 Amazon / Everett Collection Inc / Alamy Stock Photo; p47 Studio Ghibli; p49l Real Cast Inc. (Produced by Studio Ghibli); p49r Newscom / Alamy Stock Photo; p51 2002 Toshio Suzuki / Studio Ghibli, NDHMT; p52 Photo by Jeremie Souteyrat / Figarophoto / Camera Press, London; p53 Gonzalo Azumendi / Alamy Stock Photo; p54-55 Authors; p56 NHK; p57tl 2002 Studio Ghibli; p57tr Studio Ghibli Records; p58 2006 Studio Ghibli; p59 2007 Ghibli Museum; p60 2019 OLM, Inc. / Warner Bros; p61t 2019 OLM, Inc. / Warner Bros / SFG/Licensed by BANDAI NAMCO Entertainment Inc.; p61b Malcolm Park / Alamy Stock Photo; p62, p63, p64-65 Everett Collection Inc / Alamy Stock Photo; p67 2002 Studio Ghibli; p68 Photo 12 / Alamy Stock Photo; p70 1992 Studio Ghibli - NN; p71 Getty Images / WireImage / Jean Baptiste Lacroix ; p72tl A Symphonic Celebration" courtesy of Deutsche Grammophon Gesellschaft mbH; p72tr, p73t 2013 - Studio Ghibli - NDHDMTK; p73b 2013 Hatake Jimusho - Studio Ghibli - NDHDMTK; p74 Simone Ferraro / Alamy Stock Photo; p76-77 Photo by Laurent KOFFEL / Gamma-Rapho via Getty Images; p78 Classic Picture Library / Alamy Stock Photo; p79t, p79b2011 Chizuru Takahashi - Tetsuro Sayama - Studio Ghibli - NDHDMT; p80 Photo by MARTIN BUREAU / AFP via Getty Images; p81 2016 Studio Ghibli - Wild Bunch - Why Not Productions - Arte France Cinéma - CN4 Productions - Belvision - Nippon Television Network - Dentsu - Hakuhodo DYMP - Walt Disney Japan - Mitsubishi - Toho; p82 1989 Eiko Kadono-Studio Ghibli-N; p83 2013 Studio Ghibli-NDHDMTK; p85 TOKUMA SHOTEN / Album / Newscom; p86-87 1995 Aoi Hiragi / Shueisha - Studio Ghibli - NH; p88 Jeremy Sutton-Hibbert; p90 coward_lion / Alamy Stock Photo; p91 Jeremy Sutton-Hibbert; p92t, p92-93 coward_lion / Alamy Stock Photo; p94 cowardlion / Shutterstock;

p95 Photo by Jeremie Souteyrat / Figarophoto / Camera Press, London; p96l Frederic Soreau / agefotostock / Alamy Stock Photo; p96tr, p96cr, p96br Jeremy Sutton-Hibbert; p97 coward_lion / Alamy Stock Photo; p98t, p98b Jeremy Sutton-Hibbert; p99 Clemeny Cazottes / Alamy Stock Photo; p100 Authors; p101 POOL / Jiji Press / Newscom; p102 Authors; p103, p104t, p104b, p105 The Yomiuri Shimbun / Associated Press / Alamy Stock Photo; p106 2001 Studio Ghibli - NDDTM; p107 2001 Studio Ghibli - NDDTM-Toho Co,. Ltd.; p108, p109 2022 Toho Co,. Ltd.; p110 1988 Studio Ghibli; p111, p112-113, p114t, p115 Photos by Manuel Harlan © RSC with Nippon TV; p114c Photo by Dave Benett / Getty Images; p116 2004 Studio Ghibli-NDDMT; p118 1984 Studio Ghibli - H; p119 Album / Alamy Stock Photo; p120tl Hayao Miyazaki/ Tokuma Shoten; p120tr 1984 Studio Ghibli - H; p120b Imaginechina Limited / Alamy Stock Photo; p121 The Yomiuri Shimbun / Associated Press / Alamy Stock Photo; p123 Macmillan / Studio Ghibli; p123 The Yomiuri Shimbun / Associated Press / Alamy Stock Photo; p124, p125 Photo by Kyodo News Stills via Getty Images; p126bl, p126-127 The Yomiuri Shimbun / Associated Press / Alamy Stock Photo; p128bl Jos A. Smith; p128br Jeff Morgan 13 / Alamy Stock Photo; p129, p130 2004 Studio Ghibli-NDDMT; p131bl Harper Collins Children's Books; p131br 2020 NHK, NEP, Studio Ghibli; p133 Matthew Ashmore / Alamy Stock Photo; p134bl Parnassus Press / photo: picturethiscollection.com; p134br Photo by Dan Tuffs / Getty Images; p135, p136, p137 2006 Studio Ghibli - NDHDNT; p138bl Estate of Peggy Fortnum; p138br 2014 Studio Ghibli - NDHDMTK; p139 Photo by Jeremie Souteyrat / Figarophoto / Camera Press, London; p141 Photo Wendy Uchimura by kind permssion of Shinchosha Co., Ltd.; p144 TC/Prod. DB/Alamy Stock Photo; p147 NHK World TV ; p148, p149, p150, p151 2013 dwango; p152 Shizuo Kambayashi / Associated Press / Alamy Stock Photo; p153 STUDIO GHIBLI / Album/Newscom; p154 Photo by Kyodo News Stills via Getty Images; p155t, p155b 2013 Hatake Jimusho - Studio Ghibli - NDHDMTK; p156 GKids / courtesy Everett Collection Inc / Alamy Stock Photo; p157 NHK; p158t GKids / courtesy Everett Collection Inc / Alamy Stock Photo; p158b TCD / Prod. DB / Alamy Stock Photo; p159 GKids / courtesy Everett Collection Inc / Alamy Stock Photo; p160 NHK World TV; p162 GKids / Courtesy Everett Collection / Alamy Stock Photo; p164 Photo TOSHIFUMI KITAMURA / AFP via Getty Images; p165 NHK, NEP; p166 CLEMENT CAZOTTES / Alamy Stock Photo; p167t, p167b NHK, NEP; p169 Omega Entertainment, JP; p170, p171, p172, p173 Makoto Shinkai / CMMMY; p174 2021 "The Deer King" Production Committee; p175 Photo 12 / Alamy Stock Photo; p177 FUNimation / courtesy Everett Collection / Alamy Stock Photos; p178, p179, p180-181 2017 M.F.P.; p182, p183, p184t, p184-185 2017 Lu Film Partners; p186, p187t, p187b 2021 "The Deer King" Production Committee.

Acknowledgements

Ghibliotheque started as an idle conversation across the desk at work and has since expanded into a universe in its own right. We would like to thank everyone who has joined us on this wild adventure – podcast listeners, readers, cinemagoers – and also the constellation of collaborators who have helped us along the way, from our producing partners Steph Watts and Harold McShiel, who were there at the very start, to the podcast guests, film programmers, venue staff and industry colleagues who have worked with us over the last five-plus years.

We were delighted and honoured to take on this epic Ghibliverse project, and we're grateful to the team at Welbeck/Headline, including Joe Cottington, Conor Kilgallon, Russell Knowles and Julia Ruxton, for believing in it and helping us put it together.

For this book, we were also very fortunate to visit Japan for research. Thank you to Miho Oguri and Matthew Joslin at the Japan National Tourism Organization for their support and advice while planning the trip, and to Terue Ogawara at the Hotel Higashiyama in Kyoto, Sayaka Maekawa at the Nagoya Marriott Associa Hotel and Emi Sotome at the Shiba Park Hotel in Tokyo for the warm welcome while visiting the country.

Shout out to Ghibli Park travel buddy and unofficial photographer Greg Kythreotis, and thanks to Robbie Collin, Sam Clements, Louise Owen, Beth Webb, Jamie Maisner, Grace Hebditch, Paul Williams, GoblinHeath and Noah Oskow for the indispensable travel tips.

For their significant support during the research for this book, thank you to Bethany Arnold, Kate Evans and Armani Ur-Rub at the Royal Shakespeare Company;

Rachel Tregenza and Naohiro Fukao at Universal Music; Chance Huskey, Lucy Rubin and Dave Jestaedt at animation giants GKIDS; Andrew Partridge, Kerry Kasim and Anna Francis at the almighty Anime Limited; Nick McKay at Elysian, and Evan Ma and Nao Amisaki at Studio Ghibli.

As always, a project such as this doesn't exist in a vacuum, and we must acknowledge the work of the many fellow travellers within this corner of film criticism. Thank you to Helen McCarthy for the constant inspiration and invigorating chats, and to Kambole Campbell, Alex Dudok de Wit, Andrew Osmond, Ryan Gaur, Matteo Watsky and the teams at Animation Obsessive and Full Frontal for keeping us on our toes. For the WhatsApps, voice notes and conversations, thank you to James Hunt, Nicholas Moran, David Jenkins, Matt Turner and Pamela Hutchinson.

And last but not least, thank you to Louisa, Mim and Ivo, and the extended Leader, Cunningham and Maycock clans, for their love and understanding as we embarked on our odyssey to the edge of the Ghibliverse and back again.